THE SANDWICH MAKER
COOKBOOK Donna Rathmell German

BRISTOL PUBLISHING ENTERPRISES, INC.
San Leandro, California

A Nitty Gritty® Cookbook

Printed in the United States of America.

ISBN 1-55867-037-8

Cover design: Frank Paredes
Cover Photography: John Benson
Food stylist: Stephanie Greenleigh
Illustrator: James Balkovek

CONTENTS

Sing a song of sandwich, a pocket made with rye;
Lots of meats and cheeses baked in a pie.
When the machine was opened, the kids began to sing:
"Isn't that a dainty dish to set before the king?"

This book is dedicated to my three, very young kitchen "helpers,"
Rachel, Katie and Helen; and to their father, Lee.

ABOUT SANDWICH MAKERS AND SANDWICHES

Your sandwich maker is a convenience appliance which adapts easily to your busy lifestyle. Most people these days are on the run all the time. Hot food from a sandwich maker is quick and easy, and especially convenient when you only want to make enough food for one or two. The result is easy to carry and easy to eat. In addition, the sandwich maker is a handy tool for the host or hostess who wants to spend time with guests rather than in food preparation.

The sandwich maker opens up a whole new world of fast, simple cooking — hot sandwiches, of course, but many other foods: omelets, French toast, pancakes, muffins, quick breads, cakes and even pies. In addition to bread, you can fill wrappers such as tortillas, puff pastry, crescent roll dough and pizza dough. Your sandwich maker can make breakfast fare, delicious small appetizers, entrées such as enchiladas and egg rolls, and scrumptious desserts.

This book provides recipes, directions and ideas for all of these items and more.

Of course, many recipes found in these pages may also be eaten as cold sandwiches or even heated as you would a grilled cheese sandwich in a frying pan or broiler.

There are no firm rights or wrongs in sandwich making — as long as you are happy with the results. Use the recipes in this book as guides in sandwich making, but use your imagination to create other winning combinations.

We have come a long way from the 4th Earl of Sandwich, John Montagu (1718-1792) who, not wanting to leave the gaming table, asked for his meat between two slices of bread so that he could continue to play. The Earl of Sandwich had no idea that he was creating not only a new cuisine, but an entirely new lifestyle of eating, and that his name would eventually be linked to a unique way of convenient food preparation — the popular sandwich maker.

GENERAL DIRECTIONS

DIRECTIONS FOR A REGULAR SANDWICH

Some recipes require all or part of the filling ingredients to be mixed together and spread on the inside of the bread or wrapper. Other recipes simply require layering the ingredients and placing them on the inside of the bread, leaving a ¼-inch border. Close the sandwich, coat the outside of the bread with margarine, butter, vegetable or olive oil if desired and heat for approximately 2 to 4 minutes until done to taste. Watch the sandwich to avoid burning. After the first 1½ minutes of cooking, it is okay to lift the lid to see if the sandwich looks done. If using a wrapper such as tortilla, pizza dough or puff pastry, please see *Ingredients*, page 5, for cooking guidelines.

If substituting slices of meat or cheese in place of diced or grated, always make sure that you trim them to fit the bread and the machine, leaving a ¼-inch border.

MACHINE HEAT SETTINGS

For the sake of consistency, all recipes were tested on medium heat settings on those machines which have settings. If your machine has such a setting, feel free to experiment with it.

INGREDIENT AMOUNTS

Ranges are given for amounts of each ingredient (for example, 1-1½ tsp., 1-2 slices ham) to take into account varying thicknesses of meat cuts, thickness of bread slices and the capacity of your machine (which may hold from 3 tbs. to 5½ tablespoons of filling). The ranges should give you a "feel" for the proportions I recommend, but your taste is ultimately the deciding factor.

MANUFACTURER'S DIRECTIONS

Follow your manufacturer's directions for seasoning and cleaning your machine. Especially follow manufacturer's directions for use of aerosol sprays (some recommend against it) and preparing the scallops to make sandwiches without applying spreads or oils to the outside of the sandwich bread or wrapper. There are differences in the surface coatings from machine to machine and they must, therefore, be treated differently. Your machine will last longer and give you the best results if used according to manufacturer recommendations.

INGREDIENTS

WRAPPERS

Wrappers for sandwiches, appetizers, entrées and desserts do not have to be limited to breads. Vary the wrappers that you use, and if using breads, vary the bread — one of the key ingredients to a delicious sandwich.

Descriptions of wrappers (other than breads), of test results using those wrappers in the sandwich maker, and a ranking of 1-5 (5 being the best) are provided here for comparison. The ranking is based on my opinion only. Other testers' results may have varied somewhat and your results may, of course, vary due to the particular ingredient used, the machine itself, and factors such as climate or altitude. Don't be afraid to try something new and different; you may find the results to be outstanding.

crescent roll dough, refrigerator biscuits - I refer here to dough purchased in tubes in the refrigerated section of your grocery store. The crescent roll dough forms a long rectangle which is divided into triangles. If you take one rectangular section and press the triangular seams together to seal, roll slightly with a rolling pin and cut in half to form two squares or rectangles, this should fit your machine perfectly. Likewise, refrigerator biscuits may be seamed together and rolled to fit the scallops. When using one of these as a wrapper, you need to use more filling to achieve a nice, full sandwich. Underfilling will result in the top not cooking properly. This dough requires that you heat the sandwich in the machine for approximately 2 to 3½ minutes. Results were not always consistent. When it worked well, results were beautiful, puffy sandwiches. Sometimes, however, the bottom piece would be too brown by the time the upper piece was cooked. Overall ranking: 3.

tortillas, egg roll wrappers, crepes and filo - Use a much larger amount of filling to compensate for the lack of thickness. I have found that it works better to cut (if necessary) these wrappers larger than the scalloped sections of the machine. Excess may always be trimmed; however, if there is too little, the edges do not seal properly.

Brushing the outside with a vegetable or olive oil helps to achieve a more golden color. The area where the scallops close and seal the sandwich was often too brown or in some cases it even burned before I felt the sandwich was done. It is difficult to obtain picture-perfect results, but the taste is great. The one recipe which works absolutely wonderfully with tortillas is the enchilada recipe (due to dipping the tortillas in sauce). Thaw frozen filo according to package directions. I preferred (other testers' opinions differ) a basic white bread or pizza dough to these wrappers. Bake for approximately 2 to 3 minutes. Overall rankings: tortillas 2-3; egg roll wrappers 1-2; crepes 1-2; filo 1.

pie crust or puff pastry - Refrigerated pie crust (usually in the dairy aisle), I felt worked best. The puff pastry (sheets, not shells) should be thawed according to package directions. Once again, you need enough filling so that the upper piece of the dough is in direct contact with the upper scallop of the machine. You must latch the machine for the first minute or two and then unlatch it so that the dough may rise. Results varied from terrific to crumbly but with a great taste. Heat your sandwich for approximately 3-5 minutes. The middle of the top piece takes longer to cook but it will, don't give up. Overall ranking: 3-4.

pizza dough, frozen bread dough (either homemade or the kind bought in a grocery store's refrigerated or frozen food section) - If using frozen bread dough, thaw according to package directions. Roll out and cut dough into squares to fit the machine. One word of caution: do not roll this too thin as the resulting wrapper will be too thin. Heat sandwiches using this dough for approximately 3 to 4 minutes or until golden. If you use cheese, some may seep out during cooking if you use too much, or if not enough border has been left. This, of all the alternatives, is the one which I found to work the best. The resulting sandwiches took on the scalloped shapes nicely and had the flavor of "just baked bread." Overall ranking: 5.

Making pizza dough from scratch:

2-2½ tsp. yeast, or 1 pkg.
1⅓ cups lukewarm water (115°)
1 tbs. olive oil
⅔ tsp. salt

4 cups bread flour or all purpose flour
 (or use 2 cups whole wheat flour
 and 2 cups bread flour)

Sprinkle yeast over warm water, cover with a kitchen towel and let sit in a warm, draft-free spot for 5 to 10 minutes. To this mixture gradually add olive oil, flour and salt, beating until smooth. Knead dough for about 10 minutes.

Place dough in a large, greased bowl, cover with the kitchen towel once more, and place on the top rack of a cold oven. On the bottom rack, place a 9-inch x 13-inch pan full of very warm or hot water. Let rise for 45-60 minutes.

At this point, the dough may be placed in a plastic bag in the refrigerator until used, within a few days. Dough may be rolled with a rolling pin and cut with a knife or pizza wheel to fit your machine.

If using a bread machine, make the recipe on your dough cycle. The recipe may be cut in half for machines which make 1 lb. loaves (2 cups of flour). Please note that if you have a Welbilt ABM 100 or a DAK machine, you may let the machine knead the dough once and allow it to rise for about 45 minutes and then just stop or unplug the machine to prevent a second kneading. Of course, there is no harm in letting it knead a second time, it just takes longer!

Making your own bread:

Bread machines and frozen dough have now made fresh, hot, "homemade" bread available to every household with minimal effort. If you are the owner of a bread machine, I'm sure you are already enjoying the countless varieties of breads you can make. (If not, please look for my books *The Bread Machine Cookbook* and *The Bread Machine Cookbook II* — each contains 130 different recipes.)

Frozen bread dough is available in grocery stores which you can thaw and bake, providing fresh, hot bread. For variety, ingredients may be added to the dough to change the flavor and texture from a basic white loaf. Thaw the dough according to package directions. When thawed, simply knead into it approximately 1-2 tbs. of any of the following ingredients:

oregano
basil
mint
coarsely ground black pepper

chopped nuts - walnuts, almonds, pecans, macadamia
grated cheeses - cheddar, Swiss or Parmesan

Allow the dough to rise and bake it according to package directions.

If you usually make your own bread "the old fashioned way," use your favorite white bread recipe and add one of the listed ingredients either toward the end of the first kneading or during the second kneading. Continue with the normal directions.

More tips about wrappers: While you may trim your wrapper to fit the machine, sometimes it is easier to trim the sandwich after it has cooked. That may cut down on spillage and overflows. Leftover bread pieces may be saved, if desired, and used to make bread crumbs or croutons.

FILLINGS AND SPREADS

One of the main purposes of this book is to help provide recipes and ideas for your sandwich maker. Please do not feel limited to use only the ingredients in these recipes, but vary them to please yourself. Leave out an ingredient you don't like, or add one that is more to your taste. You are, after all, the one who will eat it! Besides all of the ideas you will find on the following pages, here are some tips about ingredients.

Buy chunk cheeses and grate them all at once. Store them in ziplock bags or airtight containers in the refrigerator. You may also buy pre-grated cheeses if desired.

Dice or chop vegetables all at once and store them in airtight containers in the refrigerator.

Cook large amounts of ground meat or bacon. Freeze in small amounts in air-tight plastic containers or freezer bags so you can thaw and use only what you need.

Spices can add zest to any sandwich or meal. If unfamiliar with various spices and you want to experiment, taste a small amount alone or simply mix it into some cream cheese, cottage cheese or eggs to get an idea of the flavor. Don't overlook some of the spice blends or salt-free seasoning blends for variety.

Don't be afraid to try new condiments on your sandwiches. On your next trip to the grocery store, take a moment to look at all the different kinds of mustards. Think of your favorite sandwich that uses mustard — is it getting boring? Try changing just the mustard and you have a *new* old favorite. Explore chutneys, relishes, horseradish sauces and other condiments to add variety.

A cautionary note: there are a few foods which are wonderful in cold sandwiches but do not heat well, such as lettuce, which gets soggy, and avocado, which becomes bitter.

Don't forget leftovers, which can taste wonderful in sandwiches.

Outside spreads may consist of softened or melted margarine or butter, vegetable oil or olive oil. They may be used plain or seasoned with herbs or spices. If a sandwich calls for basil or oregano as a seasoning, dress the outside up with the same seasoning in your oil. Keep small containers, if desired, of oil already seasoned with common herbs or spices. Measure a small amount of oil, perhaps ¼-⅓ cup, and mix in your herbs (approximately 1 tsp.). All you need to do is brush the oil on the wrapper. If you use an outside oil or spread, your sandwich will be more golden. If no specific listing is made for an outside spread in the recipes that follow, you may use butter or vegetable oil, depending on your taste.

If you are dieting and do not wish to butter or oil your bread, some machines require pretreatment. To pretreat a machine, simply rub oil over the sandwich scallops approximately every five to six times you use it. Again, some manufacturers recommend against using nonstick sprays as they may damage the special coating. Check your owner's manual.

To spice up any of your favorite combinations such as ham or chicken and cheese, try soaking the bread in an egg mixture and "French toasting;" see page 22 for the basic French toast recipe.

QUESTIONS AND ANSWERS

My sandwiches cook nicely but are pale in color. Why?

Bread will color little on its own accord. If you wish to increase color to a pretty golden, try using butter or oil on the outside of each piece of bread. Experiment with bread and butter, margarine or vegetable oil.

I occasionally use thinly sliced bread. Do I have to adjust recipes for that?

Yes. Ingredient amounts are given in a range. If using a thin bread or wrapper such as tortillas, you will require more filling to sufficiently toast the bread. Use the upper end of the given range or even more.

I am on a diet but the directions with my machine say to use butter on the outside of the bread. What should I do?

Using butter, margarine or oil on the outside of your bread will give a golden, toasted appearance along with the calories. It is not necessary to use anything on the outside of your wrapper, however. Your machine will probably need to be seasoned with a little vegetable oil to prevent sticking. This should be done every five to six times you use the machine. Check your owner's manual for specific directions related to your particular machine. Some manufacturers recommend against using an aerosol nonstick spray while others suggest it as an alternative to butter.

What should I do when my sandwiches stick and are difficult to remove?

Your machine may require seasoning with a vegetable oil. Consult your owner's manual for the best method to use for your machine.

Ingredients often spill out of the machine, making a mess. What should I do?

There could be two reasons for this:

1. Too much filling is being used; cut back proportionally. Experiment with your machine to find the proper amount of filling.
2. Not enough "border" is being left on the sandwich, causing ingredients to spill. Make sure to leave enough room at the edges of the bread or wrapper so that it will seal properly. I suggest about ¼ inch.

The machine is sometimes very difficult to clean. I don't want to use an abrasive as it could hurt the finish. What should I do?

Cleaning the machines can be difficult sometimes. What I have found to work is a soft toothbrush for those hard-to-reach corners. Follow manufacturer directions for general cleaning guidelines as some manufacturers recommend against using even a wet cloth. Not only is it difficult to clean the inside, but if ingredients spill to the outside, that can also be difficult to clean. As that is not the coated baking area, I have used cleansers; but, again, manufacturer directions should be checked.

When removed from the machine, the bread is cut by the scalloped edges, but the meat is not, causing the sandwich to fall apart or the meat to come out. How can I correct this?

Cut the sandwich on the perforations with a sharp, possibly serrated, knife. You could also dice the meat prior to inserting it into the sandwich. Diced meat makes the sandwich easier to eat as well.

What do you mean by a pinch or a dash?

A dash is a quick sprinkle of seasoning, about 1/32 tsp. if measured, or 1/4 of your 1/8 tsp. measuring spoon. A pinch is half of that — in other words, a tiny amount.

You sometimes use 1/3 tsp. measurements. I don't have that.

A 1/3 tsp. is a heaping 1/4 tsp.; a 2/3 tsp. is a heaping 1/2 tsp.

Can I make things like cookies and cakes in my sandwich maker?

Cakes, quick breads, and muffins cook nicely in the sandwich maker. See pages 152, 33 and 32 for directions. I have not had very good luck with cookies (or potatoes) and, hence, do not recommend them.

PARTY IDEAS AND MENUS

If you enjoy easy, no-fuss entertaining, your sandwich maker can be center stage. It's a great icebreaker, too, for those get-togethers where not all the guests know each other.

When you use your sandwich maker for parties, the preparation is easy — lay out fillings, side dishes such as salad or fruit, and beverage. No more standing over a hot oven as the guests are arriving. No matter what the time of day or age of the guests, your sandwich maker will make your party a better one.

What could be better or easier than setting out a selection of foods for a party for teenagers? They can make their own sandwiches or entrées just the way they want them. Younger children enjoy being able to pick out what they want and then put ingredients into the sandwich maker (with adult supervision of course). Breakfast or brunch, cocktail hour or buffet table are all perfect for this handy appliance!

The following menu ideas should spark your imagination.

PIZZA PARTY - GO ITALIAN

Italian favorites make a winning party combination for any age group. A cool, light dessert is the perfect finale.

Menu

Caesar salad

Italian sandwiches:

Pizza Sandwich, page 100

Calzone, page 110

Italian Sausage and Peppers, page 111

Assorted sherbets

Meatball Sandwich, page 112

Italian Cheeses, page 113

Lazy Lasagna, page 114

Italian Sub, page 103

A LA MEXICANA - OLE

You can feed them well at a get-together with a Mexican theme. If you use tortillas for wrappers, trim them ahead of time for your guests.

Menu

Tossed green salad

Quesadillas, page 72

Cheesy Taco Appetizers, page 64

Quick and Easy Nachos, page 65

Enchiladas, page 134

Assorted melon slices

ISLAND HOPPING

When you feel like you want to get away from it all, plan an island buffet and let everyone do his or her own thing.

Menu

Fresh vegetable platter with yogurt dip
Macadamia and Cheeses, page 59
Pineapple Chicken, page 104
Coconut Shrimp, page 124
Hawaiian Ham, page 129

Macadamia Coconut Cheese Puffs, page 70
Peanut Chicken Tidbits, page 68
Brazilian Shrimp Empadinhas, page 139
Fruit juice punch

ORIENTAL FLAVORS

Delicious Oriental favorites are easy to make with the sandwich maker. Add a salad and rice, and you have a meal.

Menu

Wonton soup
Egg Roll, page 148
Lumpia, page 150
Peanut Chicken Tidbits, page 68
Oriental Chicken and Ham, page 118

Chinese tea
Rice
Assorted sauces (mustard, hot sauce, plum sauce, sweet and sour sauce)

SUPER BOWL SUNDAY (OR ANY FOOTBALL SUNDAY)

Put out assorted breads, meats, cheeses, condiments and seasonings, and let them make their own sandwiches at half time.

Menu
Assorted cold beers and soft drinks   Cole slaw
Simple Easy Combos, page 85   Chips

SUNDAY BRUNCH

The easy way to have your friends over for a get-together. Arrange cheese, meats and vegetables in small bowls — beat the eggs and serve in a large bowl with a ladle. Let your guests tailor-make their own omelets.

Menu
Coffee and tea   *Omelet variations*, pages 38-41
Fruit compote   Toast, butter and assorted jams

SLUMBER PARTY BREAKFAST

Let the girls have a good time making their own breakfasts.

Menu
Fresh fruit juices   Assorted butters and syrups
French toast variations, pages 22-28   Hot sausages

BREAKFAST AND BRUNCH

You will find many old favorite breakfast and brunch selections are uniquely suited to your sandwich maker — omelets, French toast, pancakes, muffins, quick breads all become quick work, and give you the added plus of allowing small, individual servings.

Most of the recipes in this section are provided on a *per sandwich* basis or individual serving, but are easily increased to fit your needs. A few are provided for *multiple* servings and are noted as such.

BASIC FRENCH TOAST

Some people, children especially, prefer the basics. And, yes, it can be done in the sandwich maker. It is not necessary to have a filling in your French toast. Either just leave it out or, if slicing your own bread, slice it twice as thick and make as usual.

Bread: nut, raisin, white or whole wheat

	Single	**Multiple**
egg, beaten	1	3-4
milk or cream	2-3 tbs.	1/3-1/2 cup
cinnamon and/or nutmeg	to taste	to taste

Beat ingredients together and place in a bowl which is approximately the same shape and size as your bread. The real trick to perfect French toast is the soaking — let the bread sit in the mixture for a minute or two instead of just dipping it in. For best results in the sandwich maker, soak only the outside of each piece of bread in the egg mixture — only partially submerge each slice. Fill the sandwich with desired ingredients and heat in your sandwich maker for approximately 3 minutes or until golden. No outside spread is needed. Cinnamon or nutmeg may be sprinkled on the bread prior to cooking.

FRENCH TOAST WITH PRESERVES

What a variation on plain French toast! Serve with or without syrup depending on your sweet tooth.

Bread: nut, raisin, white or whole wheat

Egg Mixture: *Basic French Toast* recipe, page 22

Filling:
2-3 tbs. cream cheese
1-1½ tbs. favorite preserves
confectioners' sugar for garnish, optional

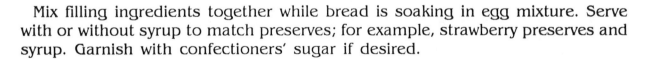

Mix filling ingredients together while bread is soaking in egg mixture. Serve with or without syrup to match preserves; for example, strawberry preserves and syrup. Garnish with confectioners' sugar if desired.

FRUITED FRENCH TOAST

A truly decadent way to start your day! You can substitute cottage cheese for cream cheese.

Bread: white, nut, raisin or cinnamon

Egg Mixture: *Basic French Toast* recipe, page 22

Filling:
1½-2 tbs. cream cheese, softened
1½-2 tbs. fresh fruit, diced, sliced or chopped: apples, pears, any berries,
  grapes, mandarin oranges, papaya, mango, crushed pineapple (drained)
⅛ tsp. vanilla extract
2 tsp.-1 tbs. confectioners' sugar
⅛ tsp. cinnamon
2 tsp.-1 tbs. chopped walnuts, optional
fresh fruit, cinnamon or confectioners' sugar for garnish, optional

Mix filling ingredients together while bread is soaking in the egg mixture. Fill and cook. Serve with or without syrup to match fruit; for example, strawberries and strawberry syrup. Garnish with fruit and cinnamon or sugar, if desired.

BANANA FRENCH TOAST

Bananas make delicious friends with French toast.

Bread: white, oatmeal, honey nut oatmeal, raisin or cinnamon raisin swirl

Egg Mixture: *Basic French Toast* recipe, page 22

Filling:
2 to 3 tbs. cream cheese
4 to 5 thin slices softened banana
2 tsp. to 1 tbs. chopped nuts, optional
confectioners' sugar for garnish, optional

Mix cream cheese, banana and chopped nuts together while bread is soaking in egg mixture. Fill and cook. Sprinkle with confectioners' sugar if desired.

FRENCH TOAST A L'ORANGE

A tasty treat for that early morning pick-me-up.

Bread: orange raisin, cinnamon raisin swirl, raisin or white

Egg Mixture:
1 egg, beaten
1-1½ tbs. orange juice
1-1½ tbs. milk
⅛ tsp. grated orange peel, optional

Filling:
2-3 tbs. cream cheese, softened
½-⅔ tsp. orange juice
¼-⅓ tsp. honey

Mix ingredients together for egg mixture. Mix cream cheese, orange juice and honey together while bread is soaking in egg mixture. Fill and cook.

HAWAIIAN FRENCH TOAST

This tropical breakfast treat is a delicious way to start your day.

Bread: white, oatmeal, raisin, raisin nut, cinnamon swirl or nut

Egg Mixture: *Basic French Toast* recipe, page 22; substitute half milk or cream with pineapple juice

Filling:
4-5 mandarin orange segments and/or
3-4 tbs. crushed pineapple and/or
several thin slices banana
1-1½ tsp. chopped macadamia nuts, optional
mint leaves to taste

   Soak bread in egg mixture, and layer with orange segments, crushed pineapple and/or banana. Sprinkle with chopped macadamia nuts, if desired, and mint leaves.

HOLIDAY FRENCH TOAST

Serve this colorful, easy treat Christmas morning for a joyous start to the day. Some may find that the mint extract adds too much minty flavor, but you may like that extra spark.

Bread: white, nut, Italian or French

Egg Mixture: 3-4 tbs. eggnog

Filling:
1 to 1½ tbs. cream or cottage cheese
1½ to 2 tsp. mint jelly
about 2 drops mint extract, optional
2 to 3 thinly sliced strawberries

Soak bread slices in eggnog. Mix cheese, jelly and extract (if desired) together and spread on bottom slice. Layer strawberries on top. Close and cook as usual.

CINNAMON "BUNS"

An adaptation of sticky buns — sure to please the child in all of us.

Bread: cinnamon raisin, raisin, orange raisin, white, whole wheat or oatmeal

Filling:
1-1½ tbs. melted margarine or butter
⅔-1 tsp. cinnamon
2 tsp.-1 tbs. brown sugar
1½-2 tsp. chopped nuts

Glaze, optional:
1½ tbs. powdered sugar
¼ tsp. milk
1 drop vanilla extract

Mix filling ingredients together and spread on one slice of bread. Close and cook. Mix glaze ingredients together and glaze if desired.

ALMOND PASTRY

A great wake-me-upper.

Wrapper: puff pastry; crescent roll dough; white bread. If using puff pastry or crescent roll dough, add extra filling.

Outside Spread: (white bread only) 1 tbs. melted margarine or butter with 1/16-1/8 tsp. almond extract

Filling:
1-1½ tbs. melted margarine or butter
1/16 tsp. almond extract
2 tsp.-1 tbs. brown sugar
2 tsp.-1 tbs. finely chopped almonds

Mix filling and spread on inside of wrapper. Spread outside of wrapper with margarine mixture if using white bread.

RAISIN NUT "BUNS"

Along the same lines as cinnamon buns, these are another great stand-by.

Wrapper: raisin, cinnamon or white bread; crescent roll dough; puff pastry. If using crescent roll dough or puff pastry, add extra filling.

Filling:
1-1½ tbs. melted margarine or butter
2 tsp.-1 tbs. sugar, white or brown
1-1½ tbs. finely chopped walnuts
2-3 tbs. raisins

Mix filling ingredients together and spread on inside of wrapper.

ALL ABOUT PANCAKES

Using your normal pancake batter, fill scallops with enough batter so that it is "heaping." For makers with two scallops per sandwich, this will be about 3 to 4 tablespoons in each scallop. For makers with one scallop per sandwich, it will be about 1/3 cup, plus or minus. Cook for about 3 to 4 minutes. About 1 to 1½ minutes into the baking, unlatch the machine so that the pancakes can rise.

ALL ABOUT MUFFINS

Your favorite muffin recipe, whether homemade or purchased mix, may be made in your sandwich maker in just 3 to 4 minutes. Spoon enough batter into the scalloped areas so that it is heaping but not overflowing (3 to 5 large spoonfuls). Bake for approximately 3 to 4 minutes until a toothpick comes out clean. I recommend that you start checking the muffins every 30 seconds about 2 minutes into baking as they bake very quickly and could burn easily.

ALL ABOUT QUICK BREADS

Banana, pumpkin, apple and cinnamon breads and the countless variety of quick breads (nonyeast breads) may be baked in your sandwich maker in just a few minutes compared to 30 to 45 minutes of conventional oven baking. Use one of the following or your own favorite recipes, or even a purchased mix, and make the batter as usual. Spoon enough batter into the scalloped areas so that it is heaping but not overflowing (3 to 5 large spoonfuls). Bake for approximately 3 to 5 minutes until a toothpick inserted into the bread comes out clean. I recommend that you start checking the breads every 30 seconds about 2½ minutes into baking as they bake very quickly and could burn easily. The following quick bread recipes make approximately 4 to 6 pieces each. Each may be halved (use 2 tbs. egg substitute for ½ egg) or doubled to fit your needs.

BANANA BREAD

Who can pass up a great banana bread?

1 cup mashed ripe banana (about
  2 medium)
1 egg
2 tbs. vegetable oil

½ cup sugar
1½ cups self-rising flour
¼-⅓ cup chopped walnuts, optional

Mix wet ingredients together. In a separate bowl, mix dry ingredients together. Combine until just moistened.

PEANUT BUTTER BANANA BREAD

A delicious, unique twist on banana bread.

4 tbs. margarine or butter, softened
½ cup peanut butter
1 cup mashed ripe banana (about 2
  medium bananas)

2 eggs
½ tsp. vanilla extract
1 cup brown sugar, packed
2 cups self-rising flour

Mix wet ingredients together. In a separate bowl, mix dry ingredients together. Combine until just moistened.

CORN BREAD

A Southern delight; hot corn bread is a real treat.

1 cup milk or water
1 egg
2 tbs. vegetable oil

1 tsp. sugar
1 cup cornmeal
1½ cups self-rising flour

Mix wet ingredients together. In a separate bowl, mix dry ingredients together. Combine until just moistened.

ORANGE BREAD

A great bread for holiday-time brunches or entertaining.

⅔ cup orange juice
⅔ cup vegetable oil
1 egg
½-1 tsp. grated orange peel,
   or to taste

1⅔ cups sugar
2 cups self-rising flour
¼-⅓ cup chopped walnuts, optional

Mix wet ingredients together. In a separate bowl, mix dry ingredients together. Combine until just moistened.

STRAWBERRY OR PEACH BREAD

Another wonderful holiday-time bread.

1/3 cup milk
2/3 cup strawberry or peach preserves
3 eggs
1/2 tsp. vanilla extract
1/2 cup butter or margarine, softened
1/2 cup sugar
2/3 cup oats
1 1/3 cups self-rising flour
1/4-1/3 cup chopped walnuts, optional

   Mix wet ingredients together. In a separate bowl, mix dry ingredients together. Combine until just moistened.

Note: Half 1/3 cup is roughly 2 1/2 tbs., if you wish to make only half of this recipe.

EGG SANDWICHES

If serving egg sandwiches for a brunch affair or your family, try cooking plain scrambled eggs and have people select their desired accompaniments. Eggs need not be kept warm as they will be reheated in the sandwich maker; however, they should not sit too long.

Additional Ingredients

<u>grated cheeses</u> — Swiss, fontina, Gruyére, Allouette, Boursin, cheddar, American, Parmesan, jalapeño cheese, Monterey Jack, Muenster, feta

<u>precooked, diced meats</u> — ham, chicken, turkey, crab, sausage, bacon, lobster, corned beef hash

<u>precooked or sautéed vegetables</u> — onions, bell peppers, hot peppers, asparagus, broccoli, spinach, mushrooms, corn

<u>fruits</u> — strawberries and other berries, cranberry sauce, peaches, pears, apples, papaya, banana, favorite jam or jelly

<u>seasonings</u> — salt and pepper to taste, marjoram, oregano, sage, tarragon, basil, salt-free seasoning blends, Bon Appetit, mint, dill

ALL ABOUT OMELETS

Making omelets in the sandwich maker is as easy as spooning the beaten egg into the scallops. Either premix the ingredients and spoon into the scallops or place filling ingredients in the scallops and spoon lightly beaten eggs on top. These cook quickly and hold their shape well.

Use approximately 3 tbs. to 1/4 cup (4 tbs.) of beaten egg. Fill egg and additional ingredients level with the scallop edge and do not clamp the machine closed. Other additions such as meats and cheeses may be added up to 1 or 1½ tbs. Onions, salsa and seasonings (salt, pepper and spices or herbs) should be added according to your personal taste. You can also use ingredients listed in *Egg Sandwiches*, page 37, and make up your own. Variations in omelets are only limited by your imagination.

HUEVOS RANCHEROS

salsa
jalapeño cheese
egg

cilantro
salt and pepper

HUNGARIAN OMELET

egg
diced onion
diced green pepper

diced ham and salami
salt and pepper

BLUE CHEESE AND ONION OMELET

egg
diced red onion
cooked and crumbled bacon or
  bacon bits

crumbled blue cheese
garlic powder
salt and white pepper

SPINACH OMELET

You can substitute broccoli, asparagus or diced tomatoes for spinach.

egg
mozzarella cheese
cooked, drained spinach

Parmesan cheese
garlic powder
basil, salt and pepper

CHILI OMELET

egg
leftover chili

salt and pepper

PEANUT BUTTER AND JELLY OMELET

This idea was given to me by my friend, Steve Vollendorf, who said this was an often requested omelette when he worked at a college omelette restaurant. It really is quite tasty and has become a favorite of mine. For other ideas, try some of the Peanut Butter and Jelly Variations, page 81.

egg   jelly
peanut butter

GRITS OMELET

egg   cooked seasoned grits
cheese

WESTERN OMELET

egg   cooked bacon
diced onion   salt and pepper
green pepper

BANANA OMELET

egg   parsley
banana slices   salt and pepper
cayenne pepper

CRAB OMELET
egg
crab

Tabasco
lemon juice

ITALIAN SAUSAGE AND PEPPERS OMELET
egg
cooked, sliced Italian sausage
sliced or diced red and/or green bell
  peppers

diced onion
garlic
oregano
salt and pepper

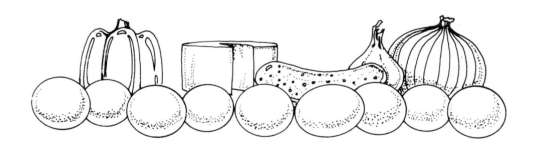

EGGS BENEDICT

A wonderful, easy variation of a classic favorite. The Hollandaise Sauce is enough for two sandwiches.

Bread: white, whole wheat or rye

Filling:

1 poached egg (for real ease, use scrambled)
1-2 slices cooked Canadian bacon
1-2 slices American or mozzarella cheese

1½-2 tbs. *Hollandaise Sauce*
salt and pepper to taste

On bottom wrapper, layer egg, bacon and cheese. Top with *Hollandaise Sauce* and season to taste. Cover with top wrapper and cook.

Hollandaise Sauce

1 egg yolk
1 tsp. lemon juice

¼ tsp. dry mustard
4 tbs. melted butter

Combine egg yolk, lemon juice and mustard in a blender or food processor. Add melted butter slowly. Use immediately.

MONTE CRISTO

This sandwich is French-toasted with the outside part of the bread soaked in the egg and milk or cream mixture. A classic. This could really be a sandwich for any time of the day but is included here as a nice combination of breakfast and lunch. These ingredients are for one sandwich.

Bread: white, whole wheat, oatmeal, cracked wheat, multi-grain, nut or raisin

Egg Mixture: *Basic French Toast* recipe, page 22.

Filling:
Dijon or other mustard
1-2 slices Swiss or Gruyére cheese
1-2 slices ham
1-2 slices Swiss or Gruyére cheese
1-2 slices turkey

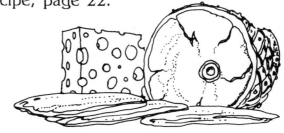

Soak outside of bread with French toast mixture. Spread mustard on inside of bread. Layer ingredients in the order given.

HAWAIIAN CHICKEN

The fruit makes this a tropical treat. Serve with either a fruit salad or a green salad with mandarin oranges, red onions and walnuts. This sandwich could be made as either a French Toast or regular sandwich.

Wrapper: pizza dough; white, whole wheat, nut or oatmeal bread; puff pastry; crescent roll dough. If using puff pastry or crescent roll dough, add extra filling.

Filling:
mayonnaise
2-3 slices cooked chicken or turkey, or 2 to 3 tbs. diced
1-1⅓ tsp. coconut flakes
3-4 thin slices banana
2-3 thin slices papaya, optional
ground ginger and salt to taste
coconut flakes for garnish, optional

Spread inside of wrapper with mayonnaise. Layer remaining ingredients between and cook. Garnish with coconut flakes if desired.

CHICKEN WALDORF

A delightful way to serve that old favorite.

Bread: white, whole wheat, cracked wheat, multi-grain, nut or oatmeal

Filling:
2-3 tbs. cooked, diced chicken, or ham or turkey
2 tsp.-1 tbs. mayonnaise
1 tsp. chopped walnuts
1 tsp. raisins
1/8 apple, diced
salt and pepper to taste

Mix ingredients together and fill wrapper.

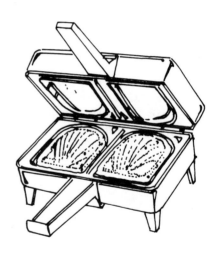

CHICKEN WITH HERBS

While this recipe calls for dried herbs, if you have fresh use them — simply triple the amount of dried.

Wrapper: whole wheat, oatmeal, white or sourdough breads; pizza dough

Filling:
olive oil
2-3 slices cooked chicken or turkey, or 2-4 tbs. diced
1-2 slices mozzarella
1 slice tomato, optional
¼ tsp. basil
¼ tsp. tarragon
⅛ tsp. coarse black pepper
salt to taste

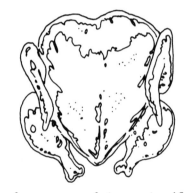

Coat inside wrapper with olive oil. Layer chicken, cheese and tomato if desired. Sprinkle with seasonings.

ORANGE TURKEY

What a wonderful, no-fuss-no-muss way to use leftover turkey with that house full of Thanksgiving guests! A real treat.

Bread: raisin, whole wheat, white or Italian

Outside Spread: margarine or butter mixed with grated orange peel, optional

Filling:
mayonnaise, optional
2-3 slices cooked turkey, or 2-3 tbs. diced
1-1½ tsp. cranberry sauce
½-¾ tsp. orange marmalade

Spread inside wrapper with mayonnaise if desired. Place turkey inside wrapper and spread with cranberry sauce and marmalade.

MINTED FRUIT

Try serving this flavorful sandwich with a chicken or egg salad.

Wrapper: pizza dough; white, Italian, French, oatmeal, or whole wheat breads; puff pastry. If using puff pastry, add extra filling.

Outside Spread: olive oil seasoned with mint

Filling:
1 tsp. olive oil
½ tsp. balsamic vinegar
⅓-½ tsp. dried mint or 1-1½ tsp. fresh
3-4 tbs. finely chopped fruit (or slices): berries, orange segments, grapes, pineapple, papaya

Coat outside of wrapper with seasoned olive oil. Mix oil, vinegar and mint together, pour over fruit and toss gently. Fill wrapper.

APPLE AND CHEESE

This is for all of those people who love apple and cheese combined. A great hot sandwich. If you slice the apple before you are ready to use it, sprinkle a little lemon or orange juice over it to prevent browning.

Wrapper: pizza dough; white, cinnamon raisin, raisin or nut bread

Filling:
1-2 slices fontina or Swiss cheese
4-5 thin slices apple, peach or pear
cinnamon and sugar to taste

Layer cheese and apple slices on wrapper. Sprinkle apple with cinnamon and sugar.

PINEAPPLE DANISH

Serve this with a ham entrée. Quantities for single and multiple servings are provided.

Wrapper: pizza dough; white, Italian or French bread; crescent roll dough; puff pastry. If using puff pastry or crescent roll dough, add extra filling.

Filling:	Single	Multiple
crushed pineapple	1⅓-1½ tbs.	½ cup
plain yogurt	1⅓-1½ tbs.	½ cup
sugar	⅛ tsp.	⅔ tsp.
ground ginger	1/16 tsp.	¼ tsp.
vanilla extract	⅛ tsp.	⅔ tsp.
banana	3-4 thin slices	3-4 thin slices per sandwich

confectioners' sugar
  for garnish, optional

Mix together pineapple, yogurt, sugar, ginger and vanilla extract. Fill wrapper with 3-4 tablespoons of mixture, add a layer of banana slices and cook. Garnish with confectioners' sugar, if desired, after removing Danish from sandwich maker.

PINEAPPLE MACADAMIA

You'll think you are in Hawaii when you eat this! Multiple recipe makes lots of sandwiches.

Wrapper: white bread; puff pastry; crescent roll dough; rye, pumpernickel or Russian black bread. If using puff pastry or crescent roll dough, add extra filling.

Filling:	Single	Multiple
crushed pineapple, drained	1½-2 tbs.	½ cup
cream cheese, softened	1½-2 tbs.	4 oz.
Tabasco	1 drop	several drops
macadamia nuts, chopped	1-1½ tsp.	¼ cup

Mix ingredients together and fill sandwiches with approximately 3-4 tablespoons of mixture. The multiple recipe makes 4 to 5 sandwiches or 20 to 24 appetizers.

FRUIT GALORE

This is a great fruit salad dessert or sandwich. Fresh fruit is always best, but frozen or canned may also be used. This recipe should make approximately 4 to 5 sandwiches. It refrigerates nicely and may be eaten as is.

Wrapper: whole wheat, cracked wheat, multi-grain, rye, pumpernickel or white bread; pizza dough.

Filling:

½ cup sliced strawberries

8 mandarin orange segments (I use canned, rinsed and drained)

¼ apple, peeled and diced

¼ cup grapes, halved or quartered

½ banana, thinly sliced

¼ cup yogurt or cottage cheese

cinnamon to taste

Mix fruit and yogurt or cottage cheese until well blended. Fill wrappers, sprinkle cinnamon on top of filling and cook. If you dice apples before you are ready to use them, toss with ¼ tsp. of lemon or orange juice to prevent browning.

FRUIT QUESADILLAS

Coconut gives this a real pick-me-up. A tasty delight. Pourable fruit may be found in some large grocery stores, gourmet shops or health food stores. Syrup may be substituted but has sugar which the pourable fruit does not.

Wrapper: pizza dough; white bread; crepes; tortillas; puff pastry. If using crepes, tortillas or puff pastry, add extra filling.

Filling:
1½-2 tbs. grated Monterey Jack cheese, or slices
1½-2 tbs. fresh fruit, sliced, chopped or diced: apples, pears, any berries, grapes, mandarin oranges
1-1½ tsp. pourable fruit
1-1½ tsp. coconut flakes
fruit with coconut flakes for garnish

Place grated or sliced cheese on wrapper. Add fresh fruit and top with pourable fruit and coconut flakes.

ORANGE BRIE

This combination of orange segments and Brie is a real winner. You can substitute peaches or papaya for orange segments.

Wrapper: pizza dough; white bread; puff pastry; crescent roll dough. If using puff pastry or crescent roll dough, add extra filling.

Filling:
3-4 slices Brie cheese, herb or regular
4-5 mandarin orange segments
cinnamon or mint to taste

Layer slices of Brie and orange segments on wrapper. Add cinnamon or mint as desired.

FRUITED CHEESE BLINTZ

Everyone loves a good blintz. This multiple recipe is for a group (4-5) and is easily divided or multiplied to meet your requirements.

Wrapper: crepes; puff pastry; crescent roll dough; white bread. If using crepes, puff pastry or crescent roll dough, add extra filling.

Filling:
4 oz. cream cheese, softened
½ cup cottage cheese
1 tbs. honey
1-1½ tbs. sliced or diced fruit per blintz
sliced fruit sprinkled with confectioners' sugar for garnish, optional

Mix cream cheese, cottage cheese and honey thoroughly. Use approximately 2 to 4 tablespoons of filling per blintz, topped with fruit. Serve garnished with slices of fruit sprinkled with confectioners' sugar if desired.

CHICKEN CHEESE PUFF

What an easy way to enjoy cheese puffs! A real treat. This recipe makes two but is easily multiplied. No wrapper is required.

4 tbs. margarine or butter
1 cup grated cheddar cheese
½ cup cooked, diced chicken or turkey
2 tbs. milk
1 egg
½ cup all purpose flour
⅛ tsp. salt
⅛ tsp. white pepper or black pepper

Combine all ingredients and mix well. Refrigerate for approximately 30 minutes (or longer). Bake for approximately 5 to 7 minutes.

BRIE AND ALMONDS

Quick, easy and absolutely delicious for brunch or as an appetizer.

Wrapper: Russian black, pumpernickel, rye bread; pizza dough; puff pastry; almond or white bread. If using pizza dough or puff pastry, add extra filling.

Filling:
3-4 slices Brie
2 tsp.-1 tbs. chopped almonds
brown sugar to taste

Layer slices of Brie on wrapper, and sprinkle with almonds and brown sugar.

SAUSAGE AND APPLE

This could be an appetizer or a side sandwich for brunch with a green salad. An interesting combination which is sure to please.

Bread: whole wheat, oatmeal, multi-grain, apple, herb, white or rye

Filling:
½ tsp. lemon juice or orange juice
4-5 thin slices apple
2-3 tbs. sausage, cooked, drained and crumbled
cinnamon and sugar to taste

Pour lemon or orange juice over apples. Spread cooked sausage over wrapper, cover with apple slices and sprinkle with cinnamon and sugar.

MACADAMIA AND CHEESES

The combination of these two cheeses with a favorite nut is really a treat.

Wrapper: Russian black, pumpernickel bread; pizza dough; white bread

Filling:
3-4 slices Brie
1½-2 tsp. chopped macadamia nuts
2 tsp.-1 tbs. blue cheese, crumbled

Layer slices of Brie over bottom wrapper. Sprinkle with nuts and blue cheese.

CHICKEN, CHERRIES AND COCONUT

The cherry-coconut combination is sure to be a winner in your household as it is in ours. Serve this special brunch sandwich with a fruit salad, garnished with coconut.

Wrapper: pizza dough; white, raisin or nut bread

Filling:
mayonnaise
2-3 slices cooked chicken, or 2-3 tbs. diced
1-2 slices mozzarella cheese, or 1-1½ tbs. grated
3-4 maraschino cherries, halved
1½-2 tsp. flaked coconut
cilantro or basil to taste

Spread inside of wrappers with mayonnaise. Layer chicken, cheese and cherries on bottom wrapper. Top with coconut and cilantro to taste.

TEMPTING APPETIZERS

Appetizers are easily made in sandwich makers with two triangular scallops which produce one sandwich. Halfway through the heating process, turn the sandwich one-quarter turn so that the machine cuts each of the triangles in half. This will seal one sandwich into four appetizers.

If your machine makes a single sandwich, cut the sandwich into attractive triangles after it is completed.

Many of the sandwiches in *Favorite Lunch Sandwiches*, pages 79-129, are also possible appetizer fare, and can be considered when you have guests coming and wish to plan before-dinner cocktails or wine with finger food. And don't forget the selections in this chapter when you have a snack attack! Here are a few special ideas you will enjoy.

CRAB EXTRAORDINAIRE

An absolute winner — guests will surely want this recipe. Makes approximately 16-20 appetizers.

Bread: rye, pumpernickel or Russian black

Filling:
2/3 cup crab meat
4 oz. cream cheese
2 tsp.-1 tbs. salsa
1 1/4 tsp. water or milk
1/4-1/3 tsp. lemon juice
1 tsp. cilantro
salt and pepper to taste

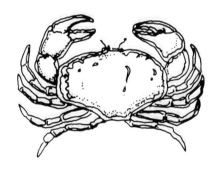

Mix ingredients together until well blended. Fill each wrapper with 3-4 tablespoons of filling.

• You can also serve filling as a dip with vegetables or crackers.

CHEESY TACO APPETIZERS

Stand back and watch how quickly this one disappears. People love it. This recipe is easily halved or doubled. Makes 24-28 appetizers.

Wrapper: tortillas; white bread; pizza dough. If using tortillas, add extra filling.

Outside Spread: olive oil with cilantro or parsley

Filling:
½ lb. cooked ground beef, drained and crumbled
½ pkg. taco seasoning
½ cup sour cream
½ cup grated cheddar cheese, or 1 slice on each sandwich
cilantro to taste
cilantro or parsley for garnish

Cook ground beef; mix in taco seasoning and water according to package directions. Simmer until any excess liquid evaporates. Combine mixture with remaining ingredients and fill each wrapper with 3-4 tablespoons of mixture. Brush outside of wrapper with seasoned olive oil.

QUICK AND EASY NACHOS

Nachos are always a favorite, and this adaptation will be, too. This recipe makes approximately 64 appetizers. Ro-Tel, a combination of diced tomatoes and green chiles, is usually found either with Mexican foods or canned tomatoes in your grocery store. You can substitute salsa for Ro-Tel.

Wrapper: tortillas; white bread; cornbread. If using tortillas, add extra filling.

Filler:
1 lb. Velvetta, sliced, or cheddar cheese, grated
1 (10 oz.) can Ro-Tel, partially drained
refried beans, canned, optional
olives, sliced, optional
chopped jalapeño peppers, diced or sliced, optional
cooked, diced chicken or beef, or shredded, optional

Layer cheese (use 1-2 slices of Velvetta or 1-1½ tbs. grated cheddar) and top with Ro-Tel and 1-3 tbs. of optional ingredients.

CREAM CHEESE CHICKEN TRIANGLES

A hot, spicy appetizer is just the ticket with a cool drink. This recipes makes 16-20 appetizers.

Wrapper: rye, pumpernickel or Russian black bread; pizza dough; puff pastry; crescent roll dough. If using puff pastry or crescent roll dough, add extra filling.

Filling:
Dijon or spicy mustard
1/4 cup cooked, diced chicken or turkey
1/2 cup cream cheese, softened
1-2 jalapeño peppers, sliced or diced
1/2 tsp. dried chives or 1 1/3 tsp. diced green onion

Spread inside of each wrapper with mustard. Mix ingredients together and fill each wrapper with 3-4 tablespoons of mixture.

SEAFOOD APPETIZERS

This is a must for those who live in "seafood country." Use canned seafood if fresh is not available. Makes 32-36 appetizers.

Wrapper: Russian black, pumpernickel or dark rye bread; puff pastry; pizza dough. If using puff pastry, add extra filling.

Filling:

2/3 cup crab meat
1/2 cup cooked, chopped shrimp
4 oz. cream cheese
1 tbs. sherry
1 tsp. lemon juice
1 tsp. diced onion

1/2 tsp. horseradish
1/2 tsp. Dijon mustard
1/4 cup chopped walnuts, almonds
  or macadamias
salt and pepper to taste

Mix ingredients together and fill each wrapper with approximately 3-4 tablespoons of mixture.

PEANUT CHICKEN TIDBITS

A quick and very easy adaptation of an Indonesian saté. Thanks to Ratih Prananto of Jakarta for introducing me to the wonders of saté. Makes about 48 appetizers.

Bread: pita (split and cut to fit), white, whole wheat, nut or raisin

Peanut Sauce:
½ cup peanut butter
¼ cup coconut milk
¼ cup chicken broth
1 tsp. soy sauce
1 tbs. salsa
⅛ tsp. garlic powder
1/16 tsp. ground ginger
1-2 drops Tabasco
salt and pepper to taste

Filling:
Peanut Sauce
2 cups cooked, diced chicken

Mix sauce ingredients together. Toss diced chicken in sauce and fill wrapper with 3-4 tablespoons of mixture.

Note: The milk and broth may be increased to approximately ½ cup each for a thinner sauce and used as a salad dressing or a sauce over grilled chicken. In addition, try pouring the thinner sauce over boneless chicken breasts in a pan and baking at 350° for about an hour; serve over rice as a delicious entrée.

MACADAMIA COCONUT CHEESE PUFFS

You and your guests will flip over this one! You may need to double the recipe. It makes 12-16 appetizers.

Wrapper: Russian black, pumpernickel or dark rye bread; pizza dough; puff pastry. If using puff pastry, add extra filling.

Filling:
4 oz. cream cheese, softened
1/4 cup chopped macadamia nuts
2 tbs. coconut flakes
1/16 tsp. cinnamon

Mix ingredients together until well blended. Fill each wrapper with 3-4 table-spoons of mixture.

HAM AND CREAM CHEESE COCKTAIL BITES

A delicious appetizer or sandwich. This recipe makes 20-24 appetizers.

Wrapper: Russian black, pumpernickel or dark rye bread; pizza dough; puff pastry. If using puff pastry, add extra filling.

Filling:
4 oz. cream cheese, softened
¼ cup grated cheddar cheese
½ cup diced ham
½ scallion, chopped or ¼ tsp. dried chives
½ tsp. mustard
2 tbs. chopped walnuts

Mix ingredients together and fill each sandwich with 3-4 tablespoons of mixture.

QUESADILLAS

Quesadillas are normally cheese-filled tortillas heated until the cheese melts. It is very common to find any and all types of additional ingredients added to them. Use your imagination and combine whatever looks good. Cilantro (a.k.a. Chinese parsley) can be found with spices (dried), also called coriander leaves, or in the produce section (fresh herb). This recipe makes 12-16 appetizers.

Wrapper: tortillas; white or whole wheat bread. If using tortillas, add extra filling.

Outside Spread: vegetable oil or olive oil

Filling:
½ cup grated Monterey Jack cheese
one tomato, diced
1-1½ tbs. diced green bell pepper
1-1½ tbs. diced onion
¼ cup salsa
cilantro to taste, optional
salt and pepper to taste
salsa for garnish

Toss ingredients together and fill wrapper with 3-4 tablespoons of mixture. Coat outside of wrapper with vegetable oil or olive oil.

- Substitute cheddar or American cheese for the Monterey Jack.
- Add sliced mushrooms, green beans, broccoli, diced cooked meats such as turkey, chicken, ham, or cooked ground meats.

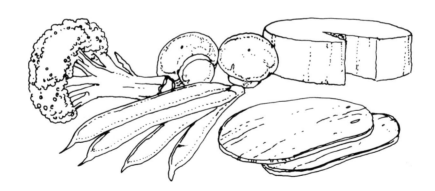

CRAB QUESADILLAS

If you like crab and Mexican food, you'll love this. A great fast and easy quesadilla and a little different from the "regular" one preceding this. Makes 12-16 appetizers.

Wrapper: tortillas; white or whole wheat bread. If using tortillas, add extra filling.

Outside Spread: vegetable oil or olive oil, optional

Filling:

½ cup grated Monterey Jack cheese
¼ cup crab meat (or cooked, diced shrimp)
1 tbs. diced scallion or 1 tsp. dried chives
⅛ tsp. garlic powder

⅛ tsp. Tabasco
¼ tsp. lemon juice
cilantro to taste, optional
salt and pepper to taste

Toss ingredients together and fill each wrapper with 3-4 tablespoons of mixture. If using sliced cheese, simply layer on top. Coat outside of wrapper with vegetable oil or olive oil if desired.

• Substitute cheddar or American cheese for the Monterey Jack.

GREEK SPINACH AND FETA APPETIZERS

Serve this with a Greek salad for a great lunch. I cook spinach and keep it sealed in the refrigerator for a few days so it's on hand for snacks like this. Makes 12-16.

Wrapper: pita (split and cut to fit); pizza dough; white or Italian bread

Outside Spread: olive oil with parsley or dill, optional

Filling:
olive oil
¼ cup spinach, cooked, drained and chopped
3 tbs. crumbled feta cheese
¼ cup grated mozzarella cheese
¾ tsp. minced grated onion
1 tsp. dried parsley or 1⅓ tbs. chopped fresh
⅛ tsp. garlic powder

Spread olive oil inside wrappers. Combine remaining ingredients and fill each wrapper with 3-4 tablespoons of mixture. Brush seasoned oil on outside of wrappers if desired.

- **SPINACH AND TOMATO**: Substitute one slice of tomato per wrapper for mozzarella and dill for parsley.

GREEK CHEESE TIDBITS

This is based on a recipe for "Tiropeta" which is baked in filo. A quick and easy variation. Makes 12-16 appetizers.

Wrapper: white bread; filo; puff pastry. If using filo or puff pastry add extra filling.

Filling:
olive oil
½ cup cottage cheese
3 tbs. crumbled feta cheese
¾ tsp. dried chives or 1 tbs. finely chopped scallion
2 tsp. dried parsley or 2 tbs. fresh, optional

Spread olive oil inside wrapper. Mix ingredients together and fill each wrapper with 3-4 tablespoons of mixture.

EGYPTIAN MINTED RICE TRIANGLES

This is an adaptation of an Egyptian recipe which is stuffed into vine leaves and steamed. This is enough for 12-16 appetizers — a great use for leftover rice!

Wrapper: herb, mint or white bread; pizza dough

Outside Spread: olive oil with mint or parsley

Filler:
1/2 cup cooked rice
11/2-2 tbs. cup finely chopped onion
1/4 cup spaghetti sauce
1-2 tbs. raisins, optional
1/2 tsp. dried parsley or 11/2 tsp. fresh
1 tsp. dried mint or 1 tbs. fresh
salt and pepper to taste

Mix ingredients together and fill each wrapper with approximately 3-4 tablespoons of mixture. Brush outside of wrapper with seasoned olive oil.

SPINACH, CHEESE AND CHICKEN BITES

A delicious combination — sure to please. Makes 12-16 appetizers.

Bread: white, whole wheat, cracked wheat, rye, pumpernickel or Russian black

Outside Spread: olive oil with basil or oregano, optional

Filling:
¼ cup ricotta cheese
⅓ cup cooked, drained, chopped spinach
1⅓ tbs. grated Parmesan cheese
½ cup cooked, diced chicken or turkey
2 tbs. chopped water chestnuts, optional
⅛ tsp. garlic powder
oregano and basil to taste
salt and pepper to taste
parsley for garnish, optional

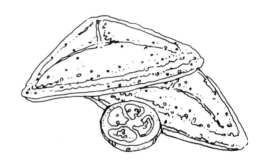

Mix ingredients together; use 3-4 tablespoons per wrapper. Brush outside of wrapper with seasoned olive oil if desired. Garnish with parsley.

FAVORITE LUNCH SANDWICHES

Lunch, for most people, is a quick sandwich on the run. These recipes are not only deliciously tasty but are also quick and easy to prepare. At most, ingredients need to be mixed together prior to placing on the bread.

Some of the easiest, most common sandwiches such as peanut butter and jelly, ham and cheese or even a basic tomato sandwich have unlimited variations. Hopefully, the lists of variations I include along with the recipes will spark your tastebuds and your imagination.

PEANUT BUTTER AND JELLY, ETC.

In addition to the garden variety peanut butters and jelly or preserves that we all use, other nut and fruit butters are available in gourmet shops, some larger groceries, by mail order or you can make your own butters. For nut butter, use already roasted nuts and place in a food processor with a steel blade. (I would not recommend processing more than a cup of nuts at a time.) Process a few minutes until it changes from chopped nuts to a "clingy" consistency. A touch of peanut or vegetable oil may be added during the processing if needed. The butter will firm during refrigeration. Keep tightly covered in the refrigerator for approximately 1 to 1½ weeks.

I've thrown in some cream cheese and cottage cheese combinations because they are made in such a similar way.

Another method of varying a plain peanut butter and jelly is to vary the bread itself. Try apple oatmeal bread, raisin bread, cinnamon raisin bread or whole wheat raisin cinnamon.

- peanut butter and cream cheese
- peanut butter and cottage cheese (with or without raisins and/or banana)

- peanut butter and raisins
- peanut butter and applesauce
- peanut butter and banana, apple or pear slices
- cream cheese and jelly
- peanut butter and marshmallow creme - a favorite of kids and very sweet
- cream cheese and chutney
- cream cheese and pimientos
- cream cheese or cottage cheese and cranberry sauce or CranFruit
- peanut butter, cottage cheese, walnuts, raisins, cinnamon and nutmeg
- cottage cheese, fruit, vanilla extract and sugar to taste
- peanut butter or cream/cottage cheese and mandarin orange segments (with or without coconut flakes)
- hazelnut butter and orange marmalade
- almond butter with peach marmalade/jam
- peanut butter with apple butter

HAM AND CHEESE VARIATIONS

Use your favorite spreads such as mayonnaise, mustard, even Russian or Thousand Island dressings. Try different mustards to vary your sandwiches a little. As always, try different breads from white to Russian black bread. Season with spices, salt-free seasoning blends and/or salt and pepper.

- Virginia ham and Brie
- prosciutto or country ham and fontina cheese
- prosciutto or country ham and mozzarella cheese
- Black Forest or smoked ham and Brie
- Black Forest or smoked ham and Muenster cheese (with or without turkey)
- Black Forest or smoked ham and Jarlsberg cheese

TOMATO AND CHEESE VARIATIONS

There is nothing better than fresh tomatoes in sandwiches. Fresh herbs really add the best flavors but dried are good too! An absolutely superb seasoning for all tomato sandwiches is olive oil seasoned with basil, oregano, marjoram, dill or mint; or even for a little zest, coriander leaves (fresh, a.k.a. cilantro or Chinese parsley). Keep a container of premixed olive oil with your favorite spice on hand. Coat the inside and/or outside of the bread. Mayonnaise is always a good inside spread, also.

- tomato, mozzarella or provolone cheese, olive oil seasoned with basil
- tomato and mozzarella cheese with bacon, ham, chicken, turkey or tuna
- add one or two spears of cooked or canned spears of asparagus
- add 1-2 tbs. cooked, chopped broccoli florets
- add 1-2 tbs. finely diced red onion and season with mustard
- substitute blue cheese or Alloutte herbed cheese
- substitute zucchini for the tomato (slightly cooked) and season with garlic powder, basil and oregano

SIMPLE AND EASY COMBOS

In place of the usual salt and pepper in all of these recipes, try some of the premixed salt-free seasoning blends. The blends may specify which meats or foods they go best with. Use your favorite mayonnaise and/or mustard or try new, different mustards.

- roast beef, provolone cheese, horseradish, mayonnaise, salt and pepper
- roast beef, Swiss cheese, coleslaw, mayonnaise, salt and pepper
- roast beef, mashed potatoes, gravy, salt and pepper (a great way to finish the leftovers!)
- corned beef, pastrami, coleslaw, Dijon mustard, salt and pepper
- corned beef, pastrami, brisket, Swiss cheese, tomato, Dijon mustard, salt and pepper
- Polish kielbasa, havarti, mustard, salt and pepper
- pepperoni, cheddar cheese, mustard, salt and pepper
- turkey, pastrami, Swiss cheese, salt, pepper and oregano to taste
- turkey, salami, Monterey Jack cheese, mayonnaise and/or mustard, salt and pepper

- turkey, prosciutto, Swiss or Gruyére cheese, red onion, oregano, mayonnaise or olive oil, salt and pepper
- smoked turkey, provolone cheese, mayonnaise with horseradish, salt and pepper
- turkey with blue cheese, mayonnaise, salt and pepper
- mozzarella cheese, Italian dressing, Italian seasonings or marjoram, with or without tomato
- chicken or turkey, orange marmalade, mayonnaise, salt and pepper

ZUCCHINI AND TOMATO

Can you imagine anything better than zucchini, tomatoes and herbs fresh from your garden in a sandwich like this?

Bread: whole wheat, rye, pumpernickel, cracked wheat or multi-grain

Filling:
1½-2 tsp. olive oil
oregano and/or basil to taste
3-4 thin slices zucchini, cooked
1 slice tomato
1 tsp. diced onions, optional
1 slice Muenster cheese
salt and pepper to taste

Coat inside of bread with seasoned oil. Layer remaining ingredients.

- For variety, add cooked, crumbled bacon or cooked, diced chicken or turkey.

THE ULTIMATE TURKEY SANDWICH

Make this on sweet potato bread and you have an entire Thanksgiving meal! I have been known to roast a turkey just to have leftovers for sandwiches like this.

Bread: whole wheat, 7-grain or multi-grain, cracked wheat, white, potato, sweet potato, rye, pumpernickel or cranberry

Filling:
mayonnaise
1-2 slices cooked turkey, or 1-2 tbs. diced
1-1½ tbs. turkey dressing
1-1½ tbs. cranberry sauce
salt and pepper to taste

Spread mayonnaise inside slices of bread. Layer turkey, dressing and cranberry sauce and season.

SHRIMP AND PROSCIUTTO

This great combination is sure to please.

Bread: whole wheat, rye, pumpernickel, cracked wheat, multi-grain or white

Outside Spread: olive oil with basil, optional

Filling:
mustard
1-2 slices prosciutto or country ham
3-5 cooked, diced shrimp
1-2 slices mozzarella cheese, or 1-2 tbs. grated
1-1½ slices tomato
dash garlic powder
basil to taste
salt and pepper to taste

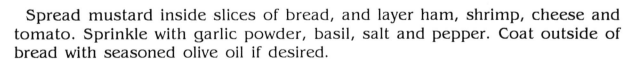

Spread mustard inside slices of bread, and layer ham, shrimp, cheese and tomato. Sprinkle with garlic powder, basil, salt and pepper. Coat outside of bread with seasoned olive oil if desired.

CHICKEN AND CUCUMBER

If you have never tried cucumbers in a sandwich before, you are in for a real treat.

Bread: whole wheat, rye, pumpernickel or white

Filling:
Italian salad dressing
2-3 slices cooked chicken or turkey, or 2-3 tbs. diced
3-4 slices cucumber
1-2 slices mozzarella cheese
1-1½ tsp. chopped walnuts
salt-free seasoning blend to taste

Spread Italian salad dressing inside slices of bread. Layer chicken, cucumber and cheese; sprinkle with walnuts and seasoning blend.

ORANGE CHICKEN

A favorite combination in a sandwich — couldn't ask for better.

Bread: whole wheat, rye, white, sourdough, raisin or nut

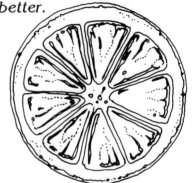

Filling:
mayonnaise
1-2 slices chicken or turkey
1-2 slices mozzarella cheese, optional
2-3 orange segments
cilantro or salt-free seasoning blend to taste

Spread inside of bread slices with mayonnaise. Layer chicken, cheese and orange segments. Sprinkle with cilantro or seasoning blend.

RUEBEN

Who can resist a Rueben on a clear, fall football day? A classic favorite — and so easy!

Bread: rye or pumpernickel

Filling:
Dijon mustard, Thousand Island or Russian dressing
1-2 slices Swiss cheese
2-3 slices corned beef
1-2 slices pastrami, optional
1-1½ tbs. sauerkraut

Spread inside of bread slices with mustard or dressing. Layer remaining ingredients in the order given.

JICAMA AND HAM

Jicama, also called "Mexican potato," is a very crunchy, tasty root vegetable. It looks like an overgrown potato and can be found in some well stocked grocery stores or Mexican stores. Cut off what you need and simply refrigerate the rest. The jicama dresses up this plain ham and cheese. Try it in any of your similar, favorite sandwiches for added crunch. A bonus: it's very low in calories!

Bread: rye, pumpernickel or whole wheat

Filling:
herbed or spicy mustard
1-2 slices ham
1-2 slices provolone or mozzarella cheese
2-3 tbs. peeled, diced jicama

Spread inside slices of bread with mustard. Layer ham and cheese; sprinkle with diced jicama.

BROCCOLI, CHEESE AND CHICKEN

Chicken and broccoli seem to complement each other so well in many dishes, why not a sandwich too?

Bread: white, whole wheat, oregano, pepper, Italian or French

Outside Spread: olive oil seasoned with basil or dill, optional

Filling:
olive oil
1-2 slices cooked chicken or turkey, or 1-2 tbs. diced
2-3 slices mozzarella or provolone cheese, or 2-3 tbs. grated
1-2 tbs. cooked, chopped broccoli
dash garlic powder
basil or dill to taste
salt and pepper to taste

Season inside of bread with olive oil. Layer chicken and cheese slices; sprinkle with broccoli pieces. Add a dash of garlic powder and seasonings. Coat outside of bread with seasoned olive oil if desired.

CUBAN SANDWICH

Here is one of the many tasty Cuban sandwiches found throughout Florida.

Bread: Cuban, French, Italian or white

Filling:
mustard
1-2 slices ham, or 1-2 tbs. diced
1½-2 slices roast pork
1 slice Swiss cheese
1-1½ slices Italian hard salami
1-2 diced pickle, dill or bread and butter
salt and pepper to taste
butter or margarine

   Spread mustard inside 1 slice of bread. Layer with ham, pork, cheese and salami. Sprinkle with diced pickle and seasonings. Butter inside remaining slice of bread.

PROSCIUTTO AND CHEESE

*A little cheesier than a basic ham or prosciutto and cheese — now **that's** Italian.*

Bread: whole wheat, cracked wheat, multi-grain, rye, pumpernickel or white

Filling:
olive oil, optional
2-3 slices prosciutto or country ham
1-2 slices mozzarella cheese, or 1-1½ tbs. grated
1-1½ tbs. ricotta cheese
2 tsp. grated Parmesan cheese
Italian seasoning or basil and oregano to taste
salt and pepper to taste

Spread olive oil on inside of bread if desired. Layer prosciutto or ham and cheese on bread. Top with ricotta and Parmesan cheeses; season to taste.

SMOKED TURKEY AND BRIE

Honey mustard gives this a little "pizzazz."

Wrapper: white, whole wheat, cracked wheat, pumpernickel or black bread; pizza dough

Filling:
honey mustard or spicy mustard
2-3 slices smoked turkey
3-4 slices Brie
1 slice tomato
salt-free seasoning blend to taste

Spread mustard on inside of bread or pizza dough. Layer remaining ingredients.

- Substitute 1-2 slices of provolone cheese for Brie.

PROSCIUTTO AND PEACHES

Fresh peaches are wonderful but frozen or canned may be used too. This is a delightful combination.

Bread: whole wheat, cracked wheat, oatmeal, multi-grain, white or sourdough

Outside Spread: olive oil seasoned with parsley

Filling:
2-4 slices prosciutto or country ham
1-2 slices provolone or mozzarella cheese
3-4 thin peach slices
chopped parsley to taste

Layer prosciutto, cheese and peach slices; sprinkle with parsley. Coat outside of bread slices with seasoned olive oil.

• Substitute pears or apples for peaches.

SPICY CLUB

If you like hot, spicy food, you'll love this one.

Wrapper: white, oatmeal, whole wheat or rye bread; tortillas; pizza dough

Outside Spread: olive oil or vegetable oil with parsley

Filling:
2-3 slices ham
1-2 slices Monterey Jack or cheddar cheese, or 1-1½ tbs. grated
1-2 slices cooked chicken or turkey, or 1-2 tbs. diced
salsa to taste
salt and pepper to taste

Layer ham, cheese and chicken or turkey on wrapper. Spread with salsa and season to taste.

CROQUE MONSIEUR

*This is **the** classic French sandwich which was the original basis for sandwich makers. Some machines are even referred to as "Croque Monsieur Grills." This is a "must-try."*

Bread: French, Italian or white

Outside Spread: melted butter

Filling:
Dijon mustard
1-2 slices Swiss or Gruyére cheese
2-4 slices ham
1-2 slices Swiss or Gruyére cheese
salt and pepper to taste

Spread inside of bread slices with Dijon mustard. Layer ingredients in the order given. Coat outside of bread slices with melted butter.

- Croque Madam: substitute chicken for the ham.

HAM AND SALAMI

Some of these old favorites are even better after they're grilled in the sandwich maker.

Bread: whole wheat, rye, multi-grain or white

Outside Spread: olive oil with basil or oregano

Filling:

olive oil with basil or oregano
1-2 slices ham
1-2 slices provolone or mozzarella
  cheese

1-2 slices salami
1 slice tomato, optional

Brush seasoned olive oil inside slices of bread and layer ingredients in order given. Coat outside of bread slices with seasoned olive oil.

- Substitute mustard and/or mayonnaise in place of olive oil with basil/oregano. Spices may still be used with mayonnaise.

BACON, TOMATO, CHICKEN AND CHEESE

Based on a "BLT" with chicken and cheese, the lettuce has been removed as it wilts when heated.

Bread: white, whole wheat or rye

Filling:
mayonnaise
1½-2 slices bacon, cooked, crumbled
1 slice tomato
1-2 slices cooked chicken or turkey, or 1-2 tbs. diced
1-2 slices American, mozzarella or cheddar cheese
basil, salt and pepper to taste

Spread mayonnaise inside slices of bread and layer ingredients in order given. Season to taste.

- substitute Russian Dressing for mayonnaise; or use chicken or turkey salad for meat, omitting mayonnaise.

ITALIAN SUB

Take that deli-favorite and heat it in the sandwich maker for a true delight. Any three of the meats would be sufficient or use them all!

Wrapper: Italian, white, French or whole wheat bread; pizza dough

Filling:

2 tsp.-1 tbs. olive oil
1-1½ tsp. vinegar
basil to taste
2-3 rings jalapeño pepper, seeded, optional
1-1½ tsp. pimiento, optional

1-2 slices salami (Genoa)
1-2 slices provolone cheese
1-2 slices capicola ham (Italian)
5-6 small slices pepperoni
1-2 slices turkey breast
1 slice tomato

Combine olive oil, vinegar, basil and hot pepper or pimiento if desired. Coat inside of wrapper and layer remaining ingredients.

PINEAPPLE CHICKEN

An oriental flavor makes this a great change-of-pace.

Wrapper: white or whole wheat bread; pizza dough

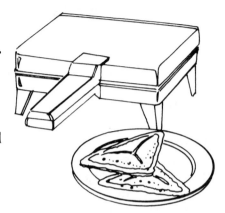

Filling:
2-3 slices cooked chicken or turkey, or 2-3 tbs. diced
1-1½ tbs. crushed pineapple, well drained
¾-1 tsp. soy sauce
1/16 tsp. ground ginger

Layer chicken on wrapper and cover with crushed pineapple. Mix soy sauce and ginger and pour over layered ingredients.

CHICKEN AND ONIONS

Crunchy is the key description of this tasty sandwich. This is a favorite.

Bread: whole wheat, rye, pumpernickel or white

Filling:
mayonnaise or mustard
2-3 slices cooked chicken or turkey, or 2-3 tbs. diced
2-3 tbs. finely diced red onion, sautéed
1-1½ tbs. diced red or green peppers
1-1½ tbs. grated mozzarella cheese
½ tsp. dried basil or 1½ tsp. fresh

Spread mayonnaise or mustard inside slices of bread. Layer chicken slices on bread. Mix remaining ingredients together and spread on chicken. Or, if using diced chicken, mix together with onion, peppers, cheese and basil.

PEACHES AND HAM

Peaches, whether fresh or canned, add lots of zip to this sandwich.

Wrapper: pizza dough; whole wheat, cracked wheat, white, nut or herb bread

Filling:
olive oil
1-2 slices ham, or 1½-2 tbs. diced
1-2 slices mozzarella cheese, or 1½-2 tbs. diced
2-4 thin peach slices
basil to taste
salt-free seasoning blend to taste, optional

   Brush olive oil on inside of wrapper. Layer ham, mozzarella and peaches. Season to taste.

TUNA MELT

This has always been one of my favorite hot sandwiches, from my childhood to present. This classic is now adapted to your sandwich makers. This recipe makes enough filling to keep on hand for a day or two.

Bread: rye, pumpernickel, whole wheat, cracked wheat, multi-grain, sourdough or white

Filling:
1 (9¼ oz.) can tuna, drained
¼ cup mayonnaise or to taste
3 tbs.-¼ cup diced celery or 4-5 pickles, diced
parsley to taste, optional
salt and pepper or salt-free seasoning blend to taste
1-2 slices American, Swiss, Muenster or provolone cheese

Mix tuna, mayonnaise, celery (or pickle), parsley if desired and seasoning. Spread 3-4 tablespoons over bread and cover with cheese.

- Substitute: canned chicken, turkey, or deviled ham for tuna; Italian dressing for mayonnaise.

TUNA, HAM AND CHEESE MELT

A great variation of a basic tuna melt, sure to please.

Bread: rye, whole wheat, pumpernickel, Russian black, cracked wheat or white

Filling:
1½-2 tbs. tuna, drained
2 tsp.-1 tbs. spicy mustard or Dijon
⅓-½ tsp. finely diced red onion
1-1½ finely diced green or red bell pepper
salt, pepper and basil to taste
1-2 slices ham
1-2 slices Swiss, Gruyére or fontina cheese

   Combine tuna, mustard, onion, pepper and seasonings. Spread on bread and top with ham and cheese.

PIZZA SANDWICH

What an easy way to enjoy pizza. Keep the sauce and mozzarella in the refrigerator at all times for quick throw-togethers. Kids of all ages love these!

Wrapper: pizza dough; white, Italian, French, whole wheat or pepper bread

Outside Spread: olive oil with oregano or basil to taste

Filling:
1½-2 tbs. pizza sauce
2-3 tbs. grated mozzarella cheese, or 2-3 slices
1-2 tbs. other additions to taste, optional: sliced pepperoni, sliced mushrooms, cooked ground beef or sausage, diced peppers, diced onions, or any of your favorite pizza toppings

Mix ingredients together and fill wrapper. Brush outside of wrapper with seasoned olive oil.

CALZONE

These are easy to become addicted to.

Wrapper: white, oregano, pepper, Italian or French bread; pizza dough

Outside Spread: olive oil with oregano or basil to taste

Filling:
1-1½ tbs. ricotta cheese
1-2 slices mozzarella cheese, or 1-1½ tbs. grated
1-2 slices provolone cheese, or 1-1½ tbs. grated
Italian seasonings to taste
salt and pepper to taste

Spread inside wrapper with ricotta, layer with remaining cheeses and season to taste. Brush seasoned olive oil on outside of wrapper.

ITALIAN SAUSAGE AND PEPPERS

A classic sandwich is adapted to fit your sandwich maker.

Wrapper: pizza dough; Italian, French or white bread

Filling:
olive oil, optional
2-3 tbs. cooked, drained, diced Italian sausage, or sliced
1-1½ tsp. chopped onion
2 tsp.-1 tbs. chopped green pepper
1-1½ tbs. spaghetti sauce
1-2 slices mozzarella cheese, or 1-2 tbs. grated
oregano and basil to taste
salt and pepper to taste

Brush olive oil on inside of wrapper if desired. Mix sausage, onion, green pepper and spaghetti sauce and spread over wrapper. Cover with mozzarella and season to taste.

MEAT BALL SANDWICH

Who doesn't love a great meat ball sandwich?

Wrapper: Italian, white, French or oregano bread; pizza dough

Filling:
olive oil, optional
2-3 meat balls, cooked, sliced or quartered
1½-2 tbs. spaghetti sauce
2-2½ slices mozzarella cheese, or 2-2½ tbs. grated
basil and oregano to taste
dash garlic powder
salt and pepper to taste

Brush inside of wrapper with olive oil if desired. Layer meat ball slices on wrapper, cover with spaghetti sauce and mozzarella, and season to taste.

ITALIAN CHEESES

A great variation of calzone or pizza. Freshly grated Parmesan always has better flavor.

Bread: white, basil, pepper, Italian or French

Outside Spread: olive oil with parsley or basil to taste

Filling:
1½-2 tbs. ricotta cheese
2 tsp.-1 tbs. grated Parmesan cheese
2 tsp.-1 tbs. grated mozzarella cheese
parsley to taste
basil to taste
coarsely ground black pepper to taste

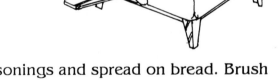

Mix cheeses until well blended, mix in seasonings and spread on bread. Brush outside of bread with seasoned olive oil.

- Substitute cream cheese for mozzarella and chives for basil, omitting pepper.

LAZY LASAGNA

Replace pasta with bread or pizza dough and you have this quick, easy lasagna.

Wrapper: Italian, French, white, sourdough, oregano or pepper bread; pizza dough

Filling:

1-1½ tbs. spaghetti sauce
1-1½ tbs. ricotta or cottage cheese
1-2 slices mozzarella or provolone
  cheese, or 1-2 tbs. grated

1-1½ tsp. grated Parmesan cheese
oregano and basil to taste
dash garlic powder
salt and pepper to taste

Spread wrapper with spaghetti sauce and ricotta or cottage cheese. Top with slices of mozzarella or provolone, sprinkle with Parmesan and season to taste.

- **SPINACH LASAGNA:** add 1-1½ tbs. cooked spinach, drained and chopped

- **ASPARAGUS LASAGNA:** add 2-3 spears of canned or cooked asparagus

- **ZUCCHINI LASAGNA:** add 2-4 thin slices of cooked zucchini

- **MEAT LASAGNA:** add 1-1½ tbs. cooked, diced ground meat or sausage

JALAPEÑO CHICKEN

This is for the true jalapeño lover.

Wrapper: white, whole wheat or cracked wheat bread; tortillas; pizza dough. If using tortillas, add extra filling.

Filling:
2-3 slices cooked chicken or turkey, or 2-3 tbs. diced
1-2 slices jalapeño cheese
1-2 rings jalapeño, or ½-1 tsp. diced, optional
2-3 slices onion, or ½-1 tsp. diced, optional
1-2 tsp. salsa

Layer chicken and cheese slices on wrapper. Add jalapeño rings and onion if desired and top with salsa.

ALMOND CHICKEN

Almonds and snow pea pods add crunch and flavor to this delicious sandwich.

Bread: white, Italian, French, almond, whole wheat, rye or pumpernickel

Filling:
mayonnaise
2-3 slices cooked chicken or turkey, or 2-3 tbs. diced
1½-2 tsp. chopped almonds
4-5 snow pea pods, fresh or frozen and thawed, diced
⅓-½ tsp. chopped onion
dash garlic powder

Spread inside of bread slices with mayonnaise. Place slices of chicken on bread, top with diced pea pods and onion, and season.

CHICKEN CORDON BLEU SANDWICH

The basic idea from this favorite entrée is adapted to a sandwich.

Wrapper: white or French bread; pizza dough; puff pastry; oregano bread. If using puff pastry, add extra filling.

Filler:
2-3 tsp. sour cream
1-2 slices cooked chicken or turkey
1-2 slices Swiss cheese
1-2 slices ham
1-1½ tbs. mushrooms, sliced
parsley to taste
dash onion and garlic powders
salt and pepper to taste

Spread sour cream on inside of wrapper. Layer chicken, cheese, ham and mushrooms. Add parsley and seasonings.

ORIENTAL CHICKEN AND HAM

The sauce gives this sandwich an interesting, unique taste.

Wrapper: pita (split and cut to fit); white bread; pizza dough; Italian or French bread

Sauce:
2 tsp. hoisin sauce
⅛ tsp. sesame oil
dash garlic powder

dash ground ginger
⅛ tsp. dried chives

Filling:
1-2 slices cooked chicken or turkey, or 1-2 tbs. diced
1-2 slices ham or 1-2 tbs. diced

1-2 thinly sliced mushrooms
sauce

Combine sauce ingredients and spread on inside of wrapper (or over meat). Layer chicken, ham and mushrooms.

Note: Hoisin sauce is usually found in the Oriental foods section of your grocery store.

"ELEGANT" CHICKEN SANDWICH

An adaptation of a commonly served chicken casserole — a familiar, well loved taste.

Wrapper: whole wheat, pumpernickel, multi-grain, white, oatmeal or rye bread; puff pastry. If using puff pastry, add extra filling.

Filling:
2-3 slices cooked chicken or turkey, or 2-3 tbs. diced
1-2 slices chipped beef
1-2 strips bacon, cooked, or 1-2 tbs. real bacon bits
1-2 thinly sliced mushrooms
1-1½ tbs. plain yogurt or sour cream
parsley to taste
dash garlic and onion powders
salt and pepper to taste
paprika to taste

Layer chicken chipped beef, bacon and mushrooms. Top with yogurt and seasonings.

CHICKEN PROSCIUTTO

This is one of the best — lots of flavor and crunch.

Wrapper: whole wheat, rye or pumpernickel bread; pizza dough

Filling:
honey butter spread
1-2 slices cooked chicken or turkey, or 1-2 tbs. diced
1-2 slices proscuitto or country ham, or 1-2 tbs. diced
1-2 slices cheddar cheese, or 1-1½ tbs. grated
2-3 thin slices apple
1-1½ tsp. chopped walnuts or pecans

Spread honey butter on inside of wrapper. Layer chicken, ham, cheddar cheese and apple; sprinkle with nuts.

CHICKEN AND TOMATO

The tomato and green pepper really make this a distinctive, winner of a sandwich.

Bread: whole wheat, pita (split and cut to fit), oatmeal, rye or pumpernickel

Outside Spread: olive oil seasoned with parsley

Filling:
mayonnaise
2-3 slices cooked chicken, ham or turkey, or 2-3 tbs. diced
1/3-1/2 tsp. diced onion
2/3-1 tsp. diced green pepper
1 slice tomato
1/4-1/3 tsp. parsley
salt and pepper to taste

Spread mayonnaise on inside of bread. Layer slices of chicken, and top with onion, green pepper, tomato and parsley. Season to taste.

BROCCOLI AND CHEESE

Serve this as a side dish to a main dish or as a sandwich.

Wrapper: white bread; puff pastry; nut bread

Filling:
2-4 tbs. cooked chopped broccoli, drained
1-2 slices cheddar or American cheese, or
  1-2 tbs. grated
¼ tsp. caraway seeds
salt and pepper to taste

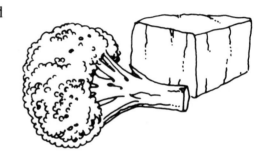

   Arrange chopped broccoli on wrapper. Cover with cheese, sprinkle with caraway seeds and season to taste.

PISTACHIO LAMB

Near Eastern in flavor, this is a tasty treat.

Wrapper: pita (split and cut to fit); whole wheat or white bread; pizza dough

Filling:
olive oil, optional
2-3 tbs. cooked crumbled ground lamb, drained
1-1½ tbs. spaghetti sauce
1½-2 tsp. chopped pistachios or pine nuts
salt and pepper to taste

Brush olive oil on inside of wrapper if desired.
Mix ingredients together and spread on wrapper.

COCONUT SHRIMP

An absolutely delicious island-like sandwich. A "must-try."

Wrapper: rye, pumpernickel, whole wheat or white bread; pizza dough; puff pastry. If using puff pastry, add extra filling.

Filling:
1-1½ tbs. coconut milk
½-1 tsp. flaked coconut
½-1 tsp. finely chopped onion
5-8 cooked, chopped shrimp (depends on size) or 2-3 tbs. diced chicken
½-¾ tsp. finely chopped macadamia nuts

   Coat inside of wrapper with coconut milk. Mix remaining ingredients together and spread on wrapper.

SHRIMP AND TOMATO

An interesting, unique combination.

Bread: rye, pumpernickel, whole wheat, 7-grain, multi-grain, cracked wheat or white

Outside Spread: olive oil seasoned with parsley or oregano

Filler:
mayonnaise
4-8 diced, cooked shrimp (enough to cover bread)
1 slice tomato
1-1½ tbs. crumbled feta cheese
parsley and oregano to taste
salt and pepper to taste

Spread inside of bread with mayonnaise. Cover bread with shrimp, tomato slice and crumbled feta. Season to taste. Coat outside of bread with seasoned olive oil.

BACON AND SPINACH

This could be served as appetizers, a side vegetable or a sandwich in its own right.

Bread: rye, pumpernickel or Russian black

Outside Seasoning: olive or vegetable oil with parsley

Filling:
2-3 tbs. cooked chopped spinach, drained
1-2 slices bacon or 1-2 tbs. bacon bits
1½-2 tbs. ricotta cheese
1-3 water chestnuts, sliced or quartered, optional
Vegetable Supreme seasoning to taste or basil, parsley and pepper to taste

Mix ingredients together and spread on bread. Coat outside of bread with seasoned oil.

CHEESE AND BACON

This is sure to become a favorite. A must for cottage cheese enthusiasts.

Bread: rye, pumpernickel or Russian black

Filling:
1-1½ tbs. grated cheddar cheese
1½-2 tbs. cottage cheese
1-2 drops Tabasco sauce
1-1½ tbs. cooked, drained, crumbled
bacon or real bacon bits
¼ tsp. dried chives
salt-free seasoning blend to taste
2 tsp.-1 tbs. chopped nuts, optional

Mix ingredients together and spread on bread.

CINNAMON HAM

You'll be hooked by this one. What a simple way to vary a basic ham sandwich!

Wrapper: white, whole wheat, cinnamon, raisin or nut bread; pizza dough

Filling:
1-1½ tbs. melted butter or margarine
1-1½ tsp. cinnamon
1-1½ tsp. sugar
3-4 slices ham
1-2 slices mozzarella cheese, or 1-1½ tbs. grated

Mix butter, cinnamon and sugar together and coat insides of wrapper. Layer slices of ham and cheese.

HAWAIIAN HAM

Pineapple and ham go hand in hand — in sandwiches too!

Bread: potato, white, whole wheat, rye, cinnamon or nut

Filling:
mustard
2-3 slices ham
1-1½ tbs. crushed pineapple, drained
¼-⅓ tsp. brown sugar

Spread mustard on inside of bread. Layer ham slices and top with crushed pineapple. Sprinkle with brown sugar.

EASY ENTRÉES

One of the benefits a sandwich maker provides is the ability to serve a hot meal to several people at different times. In this day of fast-paced lifestyles, many families find themselves juggling dinner hour to fit more than one schedule. Any of the recipes in this chapter provides a quick hot meal for one. Make a salad, vegetable dish or soup available, and everyone can have a complete meal to fit his or her schedule.

Most of these recipes (except for enchiladas) may also be rolled and baked in a simple pizza dough and served hot or cold (great for lunches, picnics, tailgate parties, etc.). Simply roll out pizza dough (one roll of purchased dough or ½ of the pizza dough recipe provided on page 8). Spread the filling ingredients on top of that and roll like a jelly-roll, starting at the wide end. Pinch ends closed and place seam down on a greased baking sheet. Cover and let rise in a warm, draft-free location for about 30 minutes. Cook in a preheated 350° oven for approximately 20 to 30 minutes or until golden brown.

CHEESESTEAK

This is based on a Philadelphia cheesesteak. Use leftover, thinly sliced steak or purchased steak slices. One of our favorites.

Wrapper: white, Italian or whole wheat bread; pizza dough

Outside Spread: olive oil seasoned with oregano

Filling:	Single	Multiple
olive oil	¼-½ tsp.	1-1½ tbs.
oregano	¼-½ tsp.	1-1½ tbs.
steak, cooked, thinly sliced	2-4 slices	½ lb.
American cheese	1-2 slices	¼ lb.
sautéed onions, optional	1 tbs.	3-4 tbs.
sautéed mushrooms, optional	2 tbs.	⅓ cup
salt and pepper	to taste	to taste

Coat inside of wrapper with olive oil seasoned with oregano. Layer remaining ingredients and season with salt and pepper. Coat outside of wrapper with seasoned olive oil.

SAUSAGE AND CHEESE

This is great for picnics or tailgate parties.

Wrapper: Italian, French, white, sourdough, oregano or pepper bread; pizza dough

Outside Spread: olive oil seasoned with parsley

Filling:	Single	Multiple
cooked, crumbled sausage	2-3 tbs.	½ lb.
grated provolone cheese	1-1½ tbs.	¼ lb.
grated mozzarella cheese	1-1½ tbs.	¼ lb.
garlic powder	to taste	¼-⅓ tsp.
salt and pepper	to taste	to taste

Mix ingredients together and fill each sandwich with 3-4 tablespoons of mixture. Coat outside of wrapper with seasoned olive oil.

ENCHILADAS

Enchiladas can include many different kinds of meats — not just the chicken, beef or beans served in many Mexican restaurants. Try crab or shrimp too. The sauces can be a typical tomato sauce, a cream sauce or even a chocolate sauce (mole poblano). While you may, of course, use an enchilada sauce bought at a grocery store, you may also make your own. This sauce may be frozen if desired.

Wrapper: tortillas (work very well due to dipping in sauce); white bread

Red Tomato Sauce:
1 (10 oz.) can stewed tomatoes with liquid (Mexican or regular)
1 medium onion
1 clove garlic or 1/8 tsp. powder
1/2-3/4 tsp. dried crushed red pepper or to taste
1/2 tsp. dried cilantro or 1 1/2 tsp. fresh

Place ingredients in a blender or food processor and process until onion is finely chopped. Remove to a saucepan and heat for approximately 5 minutes until sauce begins to thicken. If desired, use fresh tomatoes which have been peeled and seeded. Use about 1 cup, tightly packed. Add jalapeño peppers and extra seasonings.

Filling:

2-3 tbs. cooked, diced meat: chicken, turkey, ground meat (seasoned, if
    desired, with a taco seasoning), shrimp, crab, even cooked beans
1½-2 tbs. grated Monterey Jack or cheddar cheese
salsa to taste
cilantro to taste
salsa, grated cheese and sour cream for garnish, optional

Dip tortillas (or other wrapper) in sauce until wrapper is completely coated.
Fill each sandwich with 4-5 tablespoons (3-4 tablespoons if using bread instead
of tortillas) and heat as usual.

GROUND BEEF AND SAUSAGE

Kids of all ages love this — keep the mixture on hand for fast and easy sandwiches.

Bread: white, whole wheat, oatmeal or sourdough

Filling:
1-2 tbs. cooked, crumbled sausage (pork or turkey)
1-2 tbs. cooked, crumbled ground beef or ground turkey
1-2 slices American cheese, or 1-2 tbs. grated
salt and pepper to taste

Mix ingredients together and spread on bread. Layer cheese slices on top.

Note: If making this as a multiple recipe, simply use equal amounts of each of the three main ingredients — ½ or 1 pound of each, seasoned to taste. Couldn't be easier!

CHILEAN EMPANADAS

Based on a recipe for Chilean empanadas, normally made as a pastry turnover. You can serve this one as an appetizer or an entrée.

Wrapper: puff pastry; crescent roll dough; white, whole wheat, oatmeal or sourdough bread. If using puff pastry or crescent roll dough, add extra filling.

Filling:
olive oil
2-3 tbs. cooked, crumbled ground beef or turkey
2/3-1 tsp. chopped onion
paprika to taste
cumin to taste
salt and pepper to taste

Coat inside of wrapper with olive oil. Mix beef and onion together and season to taste.

Note: If making a multiple recipe, use about 2 tbs. of diced onion for every 1/2 pound of meat. Sauté both together and add seasoning.

CHICKEN EMPANADAS

A soon-to-be favorite, I'm sure. Great use for leftovers — in fact, maybe you'll cook the chicken or turkey just to have leftovers for this recipe! Makes 6-8.

Wrapper: pizza dough; puff pastry; crescent roll dough; white or whole wheat bread. If using puff pastry or crescent roll dough, add extra filling.

Filling:
olive oil, optional
1 cup cooked, diced chicken or turkey
1/4 cup diced green peppers
2 tbs. finely diced red onion
1 clove garlic, minced or 1/8 tsp. powder
2-3 tomatoes, peeled (if canned, drain first)
  and diced
oregano, salt and pepper to taste

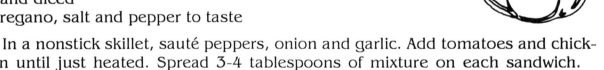

In a nonstick skillet, sauté peppers, onion and garlic. Add tomatoes and chicken until just heated. Spread 3-4 tablespoons of mixture on each sandwich.

Note: While the recipe calls for cooked chicken, you may use uncooked and sauté it with the peppers and onions.

BRAZILIAN SHRIMP EMPADINHAS (EMPANADA)

An adaptation of a Brazilian empadinha. Wow! Shrimp and coconut — what a combination. I couldn't stop eating this one. An absolute "must try." Canned coconut milk is available at your grocer's.

Wrapper: pizza dough; white bread; puff pastry. If using puff pastry, add extra filling.

Filling:

1 lb. shrimp, cleaned
1/4 cup diced green pepper
2-3 tbs. diced onion, or to taste
1/2 cup coconut milk, canned
2 tbs. Monterey Jack cheese

2 egg yolks
1 tsp. coconut flakes
1/2 tsp. dried cilantro
salt and pepper to taste

Sauté shrimp, green pepper and onion in a nonstick pan or with a little oil until shrimp are pink and onions are golden brown. Add remaining ingredients and boil until it thickens. Fill sandwiches with 3-5 tablespoons of mixture.

Note: If you have precooked shrimp, just add them in after the onion and peppers are soft. Shrimp may be easier to eat if they are diced.

- Here's an alterative use for this filling. Just as it starts to thicken but before it is too thick, remove from heat and serve over rice.

MEAT "STROMBOLI"

Italian hams can be quite spicy, making this a great, spicy meal. Keep lots of this on hand for ready, quick sandwiches.

Wrapper: pizza dough; whole wheat, oregano, pepper, Italian, French or white bread

Outside Spread: olive oil seasoned with basil

Filling:
1-2 tbs. grated provolone cheese, or 1-2 slices
1-2 tbs. diced Italian ham, or 1-2 slices
1-2 tbs. grated mozzarella cheese, or 1-2 slices
1-2 tbs. diced Italian salami, or 1-2 slices
basil or oregano to taste
salt and pepper to taste

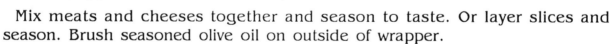

Mix meats and cheeses together and season to taste. Or layer slices and season. Brush seasoned olive oil on outside of wrapper.

Note: If making multiple sandwiches, use equal amounts of provolone, ham, mozzarella and salami. I find it easier to use grated or diced meats or cheeses in this case as it's easy to mix and keep on hand.

MINTED LAMB

What an easy, delicious way to enjoy the great combination of lamb and mint!

Wrapper: pita (split and cut to fit); pizza dough; whole wheat or cracked wheat bread

Outside Spread: olive oil seasoned with mint leaves

Filling:	Single	Multiple
cooked, crumbled ground lamb	1½-2 tbs.	1 cup
cream cheese, softened	1-1½ tbs.	⅓ cup
dried mint leaves	¼-¾ tsp.	1 tbs.
garlic powder	pinch	to taste

Mix ingredients together. Fill each wrapper with 3-4 tablespoons of mixture. Coat outside of wrapper with seasoned olive oil.

GREEK "GYRO"

Greek gyros are one of my all-time favorite sandwiches. The meat, a combination of beef and lamb, is specially pressed which makes it difficult to find. This is an approximation of a gyro which uses ground meats. Serve with lots of the cucumber sauce!

Wrapper: pita (split and cut to fit); pizza dough; whole wheat bread

Outside Spread: olive oil seasoned with oregano, optional

Filling:
½ lb. cooked, crumbled ground beef
½ lb. cooked, crumbled ground lamb
1 tsp. Italian seasoning
1 tsp. oregano
½ tsp. garlic powder
salt and pepper to taste
⅓ cup *Cucumber Yogurt Sauce*

Mix all ingredients together and let sit for about 5 minutes. Fill each sandwich with 3-4 tablespoons of mixture. Pass extra sauce.

Cucumber Yogurt Sauce:
1 cup plain yogurt
1/2 cup finely diced cucumber (I use the food processor)
1/4 tsp. garlic powder
1/16 tsp. white pepper or black pepper
1/8 tsp. sugar
1 tsp. vinegar
1 tsp. olive oil

Mix ingredients together. Seasonings may be adjusted to taste.

Note: Ground lamb can be found in some grocery stores or ask the butcher to grind some.

LAMB AND FETA

Here's another great entrée sandwich, full of robust flavor.

Wrapper: white or whole wheat bread; pizza dough; pita (split and cut to fit)

Outside Spread: olive oil seasoned with rosemary

Filling:
olive oil
1½-2 tbs. cooked, crumbled ground lamb
1½-2 tbs. crumbled feta cheese
1 slice tomato
rosemary to taste
dash of garlic powder
salt and pepper to taste

Coat inside of wrapper with olive oil. Mix lamb and cheese together, spread over wrapper, top with tomato slice and season to taste. Coat outside of wrapper with seasoned olive oil.

HAMBURGER

Try adding any of your favorite hamburger additions right into this easy "hamburger." Keep a container of cooked meat in the refrigerator for quick and easy meals. Meat may be frozen in small portions for fast thawing and serving.

Bread: whole wheat, cracked wheat, multi-grain, white or oatmeal

Filling:

ketchup, mayonnaise, mustard, or salad dressing, your choice
2-3 tbs. cooked, crumbled ground beef or turkey
1-2 slices cheddar cheese, or 1-2 tbs. grated, optional
1-2 tbs. cooked bacon, crumbled, optional
1-2 tsp. blue cheese, crumbled, optional
½-1 tsp. finely diced onions, optional
1-2 mushrooms, thinly sliced, optional
1-1½ tbs. crushed pineapple, drained, optional
1-2 pickle slices, optional

Spread ketchup, mayonnaise, mustard, or salad dressing on inside of bread. Fill sandwich with ground meat and your choice of remaining ingredients.

BÖREK

This is based on a Turkish recipe, adapted for the sandwich maker. Normally böreks use a puff pastry or filo casing and are baked or fried. Fillings range from cheeses to ground meats. A great snack, appetizer or entrée with a green salad.

Wrapper: puff pastry; pita (split and cut to fit), whole wheat or cracked wheat bread; filo

Filling:

1-1½ tsp. olive oil
¾ tsp. red wine vinegar
2-3 tbs. cooked, crumbled ground beef
¾-1 tsp. pine nuts
½-1 tsp. chopped onion
allspice to taste
dill to taste
salt and pepper to taste

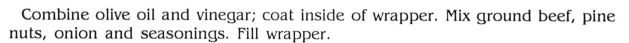

Combine olive oil and vinegar; coat inside of wrapper. Mix ground beef, pine nuts, onion and seasonings. Fill wrapper.

BARBECUED PORK

If you live in the South, you are sure to make or buy great barbecued pork. Don't forget about heating it in your sandwich maker. If you want to make your own, here is a very quick and easy recipe.

Bread: whole wheat, oatmeal, white or sourdough

Filling:
1 lb. country style ribs
2/3 cup barbecue sauce

Marinate pork in sauce, refrigerated, for about 4 hours. Bring up to room temperature while you preheat oven to 350°. Roast in a covered pan for 1 to 1½ hours, basting frequently. Shred roasted pork to layer on bread; add more barbecue sauce if necessary. Fill each sandwich with approximately 3-4 tablespoons of meat.

- Serve with coleslaw on the side or cook it in the sandwich.

EGG ROLL

What a great way to have the egg roll taste without all the oil used in frying. A true dieter's delight. A great sandwich or a side dish with a stir-fry. Also makes a good appetizer. Makes about 16-20 egg rolls (½ wrapper) or 32-40 appetizers.

Wrapper: egg roll wrapper; tortillas (I much prefer tortillas); white bread

Filling:
¼ cup grated carrot
¼ cup diced green peppers
¼ cup diced green beans
¼ cup diced cabbage
¼ cup diced water chestnuts
½ cup bean sprouts
½ cup diced cooked beef, chicken, turkey or shrimp
1⅓ tbs. sesame oil
1 tsp. minced ginger root
¼ tsp. mustard powder
¼ tsp. garlic powder
2-3 tbs. soy sauce

Stir-fry or sauté all ingredients in a wok or frying pan. Vegetables should remain crisp. Fill each wrapper with 3-4 tablespoons of mixture.

- Experiment with different vegetables of your choice: mushrooms, baby corn (Oriental), celery, bok choy or other items in your refrigerator.
- A dash of ground ginger may be used in place of the minced ginger root.
- You can also serve filling over rice.

LUMPIA

Similar to eggrolls, this is from the Philippines. Makes 16-20 lumpia (½ wrapper) or 32-40 appetizers.

Wrapper: egg roll wrapper; tortillas (I much prefer tortillas); white bread
Filling:
½ cup cooked, crumbled ground pork
½ cup cooked, crumbled ground beef
½ cup diced shrimp
2 tsp. diced onions
3 tbs. diced mushrooms
3 tbs. grated carrot
1½ tbs. diced scallion or ½ tsp. dried chives
¾ cup shredded won bok
3 tbs. soy sauce
garlic powder to taste
salt and pepper to taste

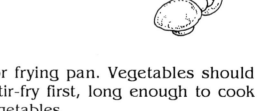

Stir-fry or sauté all ingredients in a wok or frying pan. Vegetables should remain crisp. If shrimp are not precooked, stir-fry first, long enough to cook shrimp (they will turn pink) and then add vegetables.

GARLIC BREAD GALORE

Who can resist a good garlic bread? It's the perfect accompaniment to a favorite Italian meal.

Bread: Italian, white or French

Spread:
1-2 tbs. melted butter
1/8-1/4 tsp. garlic powder
1 tsp. parsley

Combine ingredients and spread on both sides of each slice of bread. Heat the bread in the sandwich maker with no filling. If desired, you can fill the sandwich with spaghetti sauce.

DESSERTS IN MINUTES

Your sandwich maker can make desserts quick as a wink, and it's especially useful if you only want to make two or three servings. In this chapter, you'll find delicious pies and turnovers, tasty cakes, and other sweet treats that are quick, simple to make and satisfying. In addition to the dessert ideas I present here, don't overlook some extremely quick and easy desserts found in your grocery aisle.

Try canned pie fillings in pie crusts — remember to use enough filling and bake for approximately 4 to 5 minutes. Do not latch the machine closed.

Cake mixes bake quite well in the sandwich maker. Spoon enough batter into each scalloped section so that it is full but not overflowing. Keep an eye on the baking process, checking it every minute or so with a toothpick. It's a fine line between fully baked and starting to burn. Who can beat fresh cake in approximately 5 minutes!

I did not have very good luck baking cookies in the sandwich maker. It worked about one out of six times. Therefore, I do not recommend it.

APPLE PIE

Apple pie is everyone's favorite. Here's a quick way to get a piece of pie without lots of bother.

Wrapper: pie crust; puff pastry; raisin or nut bread. If using pie crust or puff pastry, add extra apple slices to make a nice, full pie.

Filling:
1-1½ tbs. cream
1½-2 tsp. flour
dash cinnamon
1-1½ tsp. sugar
pinch salt
thin apple slices, about ¼ apple

Mix together cream, flour, cinnamon and sugar and pour over apples.

Note: If preparing apples ahead of time, sprinkle apple slices with ½-1 tsp. orange or lemon juice to prevent discoloration.

● Substitute mangos, peaches or papaya for apples.

PEACH TURNOVER

Cream cheese and peaches make a tasty combination.

Wrapper: white, Italian or French bread; pie crust; puff pastry; raisin or nut bread. If using pie crust or puff pastry, add peach slices to make a nice, full turnover.

Filling:
1-1½ tbs. cream cheese, softened
1-1½ tbs. confectioners' sugar
1⁄16 tsp. vanilla extract (about 2 drops)
1⁄16 tsp. cinnamon
thin peach slices, about ¼-½ peach

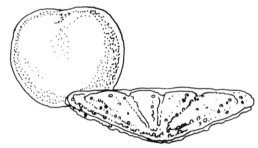

Mix cream cheese, sugar, vanilla and cinnamon together until well blended. Spread inside wrapper and layer peaches on top.

CHERRY TURNOVER

Here's another fruit and cheese combination that you'll go for.

Wrapper: white, Italian or French bread; pie crust; puff pastry; raisin or nut bread. If using pie crust or puff pastry, add extra filling.

Filling:
2-3 tbs. cream cheese
1/4-1/3 tsp. sugar
3-4 maraschino cherries, chopped
1-1½ tsp. chopped macadamia nuts or walnuts

Mix ingredients together until well blended and fill wrapper.

CRANBERRY ORANGE TURNOVER

Cranberry and orange make a nice flavor combination.

Wrapper: white, Italian or French bread; pie crust; puff pastry; raisin or nut bread. If using pie crust or puff pastry, add extra filling.

Filling:
1-1½ tbs. cream cheese
2-2½ tbs. cranberry sauce
⅓-½ tsp. confectioners' sugar
3-6 mandarin orange segments
⅓-½ tsp. dried mint leaves

Mix ingredients together until well blended and fill turnover.

PUMPKIN CHEESE NUT CAKE

Make and freeze your own pumpkin puree or keep canned pumpkin on hand to enjoy this year round. Of course, make it in the fall for that true "autumn spirit."

Wrapper: puff pastry; any bread with nuts or raisins; pumpkin bread. If using puff pastry, add extra filling.

Filling:

1¼ tsp. pumpkin puree or canned pumpkin

1-1¼ tbs. softened cream cheese

1-1¼ tbs. confectioners' sugar

dash pumpkin pie spice

1-1¼ tsp. chopped nuts

Mix ingredients together until well blended and fill wrapper.

Note: Fresh pureed pumpkin is more liquid than canned pumpkin. You may want to use a smaller amount (about ⅔ to 1 tsp.) to avoid making the filling too runny. The fast and easy way to make pumpkin puree is to cut the pumpkin into small chunks, discarding stem, seeds and inside pulp. Yes, the skin is part of what is used — small to medium sized pumpkins are better for cooking as they are more tender. Boil chunks until a fork pierces easily and then process in a blender or food processor until pureed. I measure 1 or 2 cups of puree into plastic ziplock bags and freeze until needed.

HOLIDAY TREATS

Easy-to-make-and-serve sweet appetizers or desserts, these will disappear quickly.

Wrapper: quick breads such as pumpkin, carrot, zucchini, strawberry or orange

Filling:

4 oz. cream cheese, softened
½ cup confectioners' sugar

¼ tsp. vanilla extract
½ cup chopped walnuts or pecans

Mix ingredients together until well blended and fill each wrapper with approximately 1½-2½ tablespoons of mixture.

BANANA "PIE"

The solution for the overripe banana when you don't have enough for banana bread.

Wrapper: puff pastry; crescent roll dough; white, nut, raisin or banana bread. If using puff pastry or crescent roll dough, add extra filling.

Filling:

1½-2 tbs. mashed banana
2 tsp.-1 tbs. cream cheese, softened
2 tsp.-1 tbs. confectioners' sugar
1/16 tsp. vanilla extract (about 2 drops)

1-1½ tsp. chopped walnuts or
  macadamia nuts
confectioners' sugar for garnish,
  optional

Mix ingredients together and fill wrapper.

CHOCOLATE BANANA DESSERT

Truly an easy, throw-together dessert that everyone will enjoy.

Wrapper: nut, banana or white bread; pizza dough

Filling:

1-1½ tbs. mashed banana
1½-2 tsp. Nutella (chocolate-
hazelnut spread)

¾-1 tsp. chopped walnuts or
macadamia nuts

Mix ingredients together until well blended and fill wrapper.

CHOCOLATE NUT DELIGHT

Notice this is not spelled "de LITE!"

Wrapper: white or nut bread

Filling:

2-2½ tbs. Nutella (chocolate-
hazelnut spread)
1-1½ tbs. marshmallow cream

1-1½ tbs. chopped almonds or
walnuts

Mix ingredients together until well blended and fill wrapper.

CARROT CAKE

This is an absolutely wonderful carrot cake with a wonderful, crunchy crust which is accented in the sandwich maker. Great for those evenings when the sweet tooth hits but you don't want to bake a whole cake! Makes 2 to 3 servings.

½ cup grated carrot
¼ cup vegetable oil
1 egg
½ cup sugar
½ tsp. cinnamon
⅓ tsp. baking soda
½ cup self-rising flour
¼ cup oats, regular or quick
2 tbs. chopped walnuts, optional

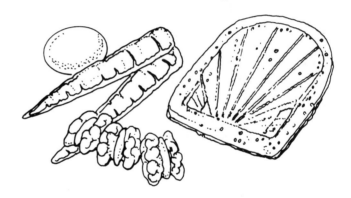

Beat together carrot, oil and egg. Add sugar, cinnamon, baking soda, flour and oats; mix well. Add walnuts if desired. Spoon batter into scallops until full but not overflowing. Bake for approximately 5 to 7 minutes, checking often for doneness.

PUMPKIN OATMEAL CAKE

You can't beat this for ease and quickness when you want something sweet. Great in the fall if using fresh, cooked pumpkin. Makes 2 or 3 servings.

½ cup canned or cooked, pureed pumpkin
2 tbs. vegetable oil
1 egg
⅓ cup brown sugar, firmly packed
¾ tsp. pumpkin pie spice
½ cup biscuit mix
⅓ cup oats, regular or quick
2-3 tbs. chopped walnuts or pecans, optional

Beat together pumpkin, oil and egg. Add brown sugar, pumpkin pie spice, biscuit mix and oats; mix well. Add nuts if desired. Spoon batter into scallops until full but not overflowing. Bake for approximately 4 to 5 minutes, checking often for doneness.

APPLE SPICE "PIE"

A delightful cross between an apple pie and spice cake.

Wrapper: pie crust; puff pastry; white bread. If using puff pastry, add extra filling.
Filling:

1½-2 tbs. applesauce
pumpkin pie spice to taste
½-¾ tsp. brown sugar, firmly packed

2 tsp.-1 tbs. all purpose flour
1-1½ tbs. chopped walnuts, optional
1-1½ tbs. raisins, optional

Season applesauce with pumpkin pie spice to taste. Add sugar, flour, walnuts and raisins if desired. Bake for approximately 3 to 4 minutes.

HAWAIIAN DELIGHT

The chocolate, coconut and macadamia combination will hook you!

Wrapper: pie crust; crescent roll dough; puff pastry; white bread. If using crescent roll dough or puff pastry, add extra filling.
Filling:

1½-2 tbs. coconut milk
⅔-1 tsp. confectioners' sugar

1-1¼ tbs. coconut flakes
1-1½ tbs. chopped macamadia nuts

Mix ingredients together and fill wrapper.

SUGARED PUMPKIN GOODIES

These pumpkin treats are sure to make a hit during the fall and holiday season.

Wrapper: pie crust; crescent roll or biscuit dough; puff pastry; white bread. Use extra filling unless using white bread.

Filling:
2-3 tbs. canned or cooked, pureed pumpkin
1-1½ tbs. brown sugar
1-1½ tbs. chopped walnuts
2-3 tsp. raisins
pinch pumpkin pie spice

Mix ingredients together and fill wrapper.

NUT TREAT

Try using any combination of your favorite nuts in this delightful treat.

Wrapper: cinnamon raisin bread; puff pastry; crescent roll dough. If using puff pastry or crescent roll dough, add extra filling.

Filling:

2-3 tbs. finely chopped walnuts

2 tsp.-1 tbs. finely chopped almonds

1½-2 tsp. confectioners' sugar

1-1⅓ tbs. cream cheese

Mix all ingredients together until well blended; fill wrapper.

AMARETTO CHOCOLATE TRIANGLES

What a treat! Sure to please the chocolate lover.

Wrapper: crescent roll dough; puff pastry; pie crust; white bread. If using puff pastry or pie crust, add extra filling.

Filling:

2-3 tbs. Nutella (chocolate-hazelnut spread)

2-2½ tsp. Amaretto liqueur

1-1½ tbs. finely chopped almonds

2-3 tsp. confectioners' sugar

Mix all ingredients together and fill wrapper.

INDEX

SERVE CREATIVE, EASY, NUTRITIOUS MEALS WITH NITTY GRITTY® COOKBOOKS

The Bread Machine Cookbook
The Bread Machine Cookbook II
The Sandwich Maker Cookbook
The Juicer Book
Bread Baking (traditional),
  revised
The Kid's Cookbook, revised
The Kid's Microwave Cookbook
15-Minute Meals for 1 or 2
Recipes for the 9x13 Pan
Turkey, the Magic Ingredient
Chocolate Cherry Tortes and
  Other Lowfat Delights
Lowfat American Favorites
Lowfat International Cuisine

The Hunk Cookbook
Now That's Italian!
Fabulous Fiber Cookery
Low Salt, Low Sugar, Low Fat
  Desserts
What's for Breakfast?
Healthy Cooking on the Run
Healthy Snacks for Kids
Creative Soups & Salads
Quick & Easy Pasta Recipes
Muffins, Nut Breads and More
The Barbecue Book
The Wok
New Ways with Your Wok
Quiche & Soufflé Cookbook

Easy Microwave Cooking
Cooking for 1 or 2
Meals in Minutes
New Ways to Enjoy Chicken
Favorite Seafood Recipes
No Salt, No Sugar, No Fat
  Cookbook
New International Fondue
  Cookbook
Extra-Special Crockery Pot
  Recipes
Favorite Cookie Recipes
Authentic Mexican Cooking
Fisherman's Wharf Cookbook
The Creative Lunch Box

Write or call for our free catalog.
Bristol Publishing Enterprises, Inc.
P.O. Box 1737, San Leandro, CA 94577
(800)346-4889; in California (510)895-4461